Organizational
Troubleshooters

James T. Ziegenfuss, Jr.

Organizational Troubleshooters

Resolving Problems with Customers and Employees

HD
30.29
.Z54
1988
West

Jossey-Bass Publishers

San Francisco • London • 1988

ORGANIZATIONAL TROUBLESHOOTERS
Resolving Problems with Customers and Employees
by James T. Ziegenfuss, Jr.

Copyright © 1988 by: Jossey-Bass Inc., Publishers
350 Sansome Street
San Francisco, California 94104

&

Jossey-Bass Limited
28 Banner Street
London EC1Y 8QE

Copyright under International, Pan American, and
Universal Copyright Conventions. All rights
reserved. No part of this book may be reproduced
in any form—except for brief quotation (not to
exceed 1,000 words) in a review or professional
work—without permission in writing from the publishers.

Library of Congress Cataloging-in-Publication Data

Ziegenfuss, James T.
  Organizational troubleshooters.

  (The Jossey-Bass management series)
  Bibliography: p.
  Includes index.
  1. Problem solving. 2. Management. 3. Personnel
management. 4. Customer relations. 5. Ombudsman.
I. Title. II. Series.
HD30.29.Z54   1988   658.4   87-46340
ISBN 1-55542-095-8 (alk. paper)

Manufactured in the United States of America

The paper in this book meets the guidelines for
permanence and durability of the Committee on
Production Guidelines for Book Longevity of the
Council on Library Resources.

JACKET DESIGN BY WILLI BAUM

FIRST EDITION

Code 8822

The Jossey-Bass Management Series

Contents

Foreword

Are you an overworked, hard-pressed manager? How much time do you spend handling complaints and having to deal with people problems? The average manager spends at least half of his or her work time at such pursuits; many spend quite a lot more than this. Would you like to be able to delegate some of this work? Would you like to have an in-house consultant to help you when you are on your own?

This book is important because it gives us all new ways to think about a very old profession. The ancient profession of troubleshooting and complaint handling is becoming formalized and far more sophisticated—and far more common—in North American companies and public institutions. CEOs, human resource managers, and every kind of line manager will welcome the chance, which this book provides, to think systematically about troubleshooting and about ombudsmanry.

Please do not be put off by one of the troubleshooter labels, the term *ombudsman*. All of us who are ombudspeople know the term itself is strange. (We get hilarious letters: "Dear Ombuddy . . ."; "Dear Embalmsman. . . .") People just keep using the word because it has become the generic term for a neutral or impartial conflict manager in a sea of "brand names." These brand names may look very different: Work Problems Counselor, Internal Mediator, Liaison Manager, Personnel Communications Manager, Long-Term Care Ombudsman. But in terms of values, ethics, and practices, ombudspeople and troubleshooters have a great deal in common. This is what this book is about.

All professional neutrals will have an interest in this book, as we participate in the growing professionalism of our trade. I estimate that there may be as many as 8,000 ombudsman-like practitioners in North America. In addition, there are a great many more informal "troubleshooters." No two are exactly the same; indeed there is almost no descriptive sentence that is true for all of us who consider ourselves ombudspeople or ombudsman-like neutrals. Nevertheless we are a swiftly growing profession (now exceeding in number all the other professionals of "neutrals").

A major significance of this book lies in the contribution of its subject matter to improved productivity in North American management, both private and public. Wherever you read, wherever you listen, you will find discussions of the new industrial relations, of employee involvement, of participatory management, of increasing interest in the needs of the client/consumer—in order to be competitive. The advent of ombudspeople and troubleshooters in the field of complaint and conflict management is one important strand in the broad sweep of management responses to new markets and new populations of workers.

New markets and new populations there certainly are. Aging North Americans need long-term care ombudspeople. Our increasingly heterogeneous work force requires new conflict managers. (Up to 90 percent of all new workers in the United States in the 1990s will be women, minorities, immigrants, "nontraditional" workers.) Prisons, mental health facilities, and health care institutions are ever more needed and so are ombudspeople, to serve them. Private industry is committed to successful competition in *world* markets. But increasing heterogeneity and an increasing commitment to meet the interests of consumers and clients of different values breed disputes and complaints; hence the long-term significance of this book.

Each reader will calculate for herself or himself the cost-effectiveness of troubleshooters. Practitioners of the profession are also very much engaged in this issue, as we seek to promote the welfare of employees and managers, to foster productivity, and to reduce costs. This book helps in laying out the details.

Jim Ziegenfuss has been a familiar and cherished colleague for dozens of corporate and health care ombudspeople, and for hundreds of troubleshooters. For years he has explored our domain, written scholarly books and practical articles about us, visited in our offices, pored over our data, sent us questionnaires, and attended our working conferences. He has been an extraordinarily popular teacher in the classroom; he is trusted, also, by practitioners. Jim has, in fact, been one of only a tiny handful of nonpractitioners trusted and accepted by ombudspeople themselves to "listen in" on our work. He asks questions that we ourselves find important; he cares about the success of our employers and of our clients, and we appreciate it.

Cambridge, Massachusetts   Mary P. Rowe, Ph.D.
March 1988   *Special Assistant to the*
          President of MIT
          Adjunct Professor of
          Management
          The MIT Sloan School of
          Management

          Cofounder and Past President
          Corporate Ombudsman
          Association

Preface

All organizations have employees and customers and all organizations have employee and customer complaints. Only organizations committed to a search for excellence listen to and respond to these complaints, however. These organizations recognize the personal and corporate benefits derived from solving problems. Who are the organization's problem solvers and how do they work? This book considers the purposes, activities, and benefits of troubleshooters as problem solvers.

Troubleshooters are important because of their potential impact on three key areas in companies and other institutions: quality of working life, productivity, and organizational development. They could be said to be an organizational development tool, since they contribute to the quality of working life and simultaneously provide a means for removing barriers to productivity. The existence of troubleshooting also suggests that management understands that all organizations have problems and that some attempt must be made to assist members in resolving them. In this respect, organizations with troubleshooter programs are actually on the cutting edge of innovative management strategies.

A comment on my own background is appropriate. I have been involved in the development of troubleshooter programs directly for the past eight years. Previously, some thirteen or fourteen years ago, I became interested in the notion of how we use consumer and employee feedback to develop systems, particularly through organizational evaluations (analysis of the status of the organization). At that time, I designed consumer and employee feedback into formal organization and management reviews. More recently, my research has been reported in various journal articles and in a book entitled *Patient/Client/Employee Complaint Programs: An Organizational Systems Model* (1985c). I have also been most fortunate these last few years to become part of an emerging national network that has recently incorporated and has identified itself as the Corporate Ombudsman Association.

In talking to colleagues in this association, I have found that there is a barrier to open discussion of troubleshooting activities. Troubleshooters recognize the sensitive nature of the cases they are brought in to solve and the concerns that their corporations have for absolute secrecy about the fact that problems and problem solvers exist. This is understandable, but unfortunately it becomes an obstacle to widespread recognition of the troubleshooter concept.

What is required, therefore, is additional analysis and publicizing of the concept. Analysts in universities can address the notion without fear that admitting there are problems will taint the corporate image (despite the fact that *all* organizations have problems). Since health care and university troubleshooters— labeled ombudsmen—are generally well accepted, I can report on them from an academic perspective and on the basis of my previous program design and development experience. My orientation is a general one; I am not directing the discussion toward a single program or program design, but instead am trying to capture the essence of what troubleshooters do.

The book is written in the first place for troubleshooters in the diverse fields in which they are now at work—business and industry, government, health care, education, journalism, long-term care, and corrections. It is intended to assist them in understanding their unique contributions to the organization and to describe their work in a way that crosses organizational boundaries.

Second, the book is written for executives in private and public organizations. Many executives are now aware of the troubleshooter's uses and benefits. Many more executives would start a program if they knew what the concept was all about. This book is designed to clarify this for them.

Last, the book is written for students in management and

administration programs, particularly in human resource courses. Troubleshooting is rapidly being recognized in the personnel field as a concept to know about. The book should also be useful in courses on labor relations in both management and law schools. Conflict resolution and avoidance are the essence of labor relations.

The book is organized as follows. Chapter One indicates why there is a need for troubleshooters. Chapter Two defines trouble-shooters and links them to a history of problem solvers such as ombudsmen. The third chapter examines the nature of the trouble-shooter's job. Chapter Four takes the reader through the process of program creation, and includes a sample analysis prepared by a program planning team. Authority and power are the topics of the fifth chapter; these are the basis for the troubleshooter's ability to intervene and to create solutions to problems. Chapter Six relates troubleshooting to management and organizationwide communication. Chapter Seven presents a day in the life of a troubleshooter as one means of informing readers of the nature of the daily work. Chapter Eight presents sample cases of both employee and customer troubleshooters. Chapter Nine reviews how the performance of troubleshooters is monitored and controlled. Chapter Ten presents the benefits of troubleshooters—what the payoffs are for individuals and companies. The final chapter reviews where to go from here. How will troubleshooters and companies progress in the future? It can be seen that the book is designed to take the reader from the need for troubleshooters through their purpose and description to cases and control, a complete design review that makes program development possible.

I have tried to represent as clearly and concisely as possible the actual nature of troubleshooting work. My admiration for those engaged is great, but not greater than my belief that some type of troubleshooter should be at work in all organizations. Any organization that is concerned about fairness, about continued learning, and about organizational development will surely be interested in this notion.

Acknowledgments

I have been thinking about upward feedback and organizational problem solving since 1972, when I began collaboration with David

Lasky, an industrial-organizational psychologist. He wanted me to listen to consumers to learn what the problems and successes of hospitals and other institutions actually were, not what we thought they were. Combining graduate training in psychology and management further convinced me of the appropriateness of this perspective. This notion of communications and listening was deepened in my training in the doctoral program in Social Systems Sciences at the Wharton School of the University of Pennsylvania. My advisors, Eric Trist and Peter Davis, would see this as I do, as a social and a technical system intervention. Russell Ackoff has regarded ombudsmen as a communication tool and has advocated their use in major private corporations. At the Center for the Quality of Working Life at Pennsylvania State University, my colleague Rupert Chisholm and I also advocate this thinking for private corporations.

In the past four years, I have come to know Mary Rowe, ombudsman at MIT and cofounder of the Corporate Ombudsman Association. I have great admiration for her work and very much appreciate her support for my endeavors in this area. I would also like to thank the Corporate Ombudsman Association for its support of my research over the past two years.

I have learned much from personal visits to corporate ombudsmen: Beth Lewis at Control Data, Clair Balfour at the *Montreal Gazette,* Richard Daignault at Air Canada, Kathleen Zicat at the National Bank of Canada, and Patricia O'Rourke at Royal Victoria Hospital.

Moreover, I would like to express my appreciation to six troubleshooters for careful and helpful reviews: Tony Perneski at AT&T, Jeanne Scott at Pennsylvania Blue Shield, Monique Guenin at the Civil Rights Compliance Department of the Pennsylvania Department of Public Welfare, Donna Simpson at General Dynamics, Jan Charette of the Pennsylvania Welfare Department's Office of Client Rights, and Mary Rowe at MIT. I am very much indebted to Wendy Kauffman for help with manuscript preparation, to Julie Kandrysawtz for research assistance, and to Elizabeth Judd for excellent editorial advice. And I am especially grateful for the advice of William Hicks, Management Series Publisher at Jossey-Bass. His comments have been most helpful.

I am especially indebted to two colleagues, Jan Charette and Monique Guenin. The three of us worked hard to design and develop a health care ombudsman program over a six-year period. The effort has been most rewarding. During this time, we have gone through all of the design and development processes identified here. This work has been demanding, but certainly less so than trouble-shooting itself.

The benefits to individuals and to their organizations make the investment in design and troubleshooting work well worth the effort.

Harrisburg, Pennsylvania   James T. Ziegenfuss, Jr.
April 1988

The Author

James T. Ziegenfuss, Jr., is associate professor of management in the graduate program in public administration and also serves as associate director of the Center for the Quality of Working Life at Pennsylvania State University. He received his B.A. degree in English from the University of Maryland (1969), his M.A. degree in psychology from Temple University (1972), his M.P.A. degree from Pennsylvania State University (1977), and his Ph.D. degree in social systems sciences from the Wharton School, University of Pennsylvania (1980).

For ten years before joining the faculty, Ziegenfuss worked in organization analysis, planning, and development in both public and private organizations, publishing results of the applied research. His current research interests are in organizational analysis and organizational development, particularly consumer and employee feedback and strategic planning.

He is author of numerous articles and eight books, including *Patients' Rights and Organizational Models* (1983a), *Patients' Rights and Professional Practice* (1983b), *Patient/Client/Employee Complaint Programs: An Organizational Systems Model* (1985c), *Behavioral Scientists in Courts and Corrections* (1985), and *DRGs and Hospital Impact: An Organizational Systems Analysis* (1985).

Ziegenfuss is an active consultant to private and public organizations, and serves on the boards of several organizations. His current projects involve the design of complaint programs, strategic planning, process consultation, and the creation of innovative cultures.

Organizational
Troubleshooters

1

The Need for Troubleshooters and Problem Solvers in Organizations

Are there any organizations without employee or customer problems? No! No company is perfect! Every organization, large or small, public or private, experiences problems between management and employees. And in real life, consumers of the organization's goods and services complain about them. Often the problems entail questions of individual interest versus organizational interest, including whether there is equity in treatment. Is an employee's layoff fair or is it not? Does the corporation respond to customer complaints? Can a patient get information about the bill? These stories should sound familiar:

COLLEAGUE 1: I just paid $525 for a lawn mower. I used it six times, and the engine blew up. When I called to complain, no one would listen. They said to stick it in my car and drive it in myself if I wanted it fixed. It doesn't even fit and I won't do it anyway.

COLLEAGUE 2: You think that's bad. Boy, did I get bad news in one hell of a way. My division manager said I was being transferred to St. Louis in three weeks. He said no discussion and walked out. I don't even know what my new status will be.

There is a long history of attempts to solve "people problems"—which are present in all organizations. During the early years of our industrial and management history, problem resolution

1

was generally in favor of the organization. "Let the buyer beware" was the message for the customer. Most employees were glad to have jobs. They were not inclined to make their complaints public. With the emergence of unions, formalized processes to address complaints were developed. These internal grievance mechanisms were thought to increase fairness and to improve conflict resolution. And they did!

In recent years, however, the approach to problem solving has increasingly involved the courts—for both employees and consumers. It is hardly news that litigation in almost every area of American life has risen dramatically, and litigation in employee and consumer relations in particular has experienced a dramatic increase. Labor relations and labor conflict law practice is certainly a growth industry, but one with very high human and financial costs. This is encouraging a search for alternative mechanisms for dispute resolution. Public and private organizations are simply finding that it is far too expensive to have in-house and private firm attorneys solve organization/employee and organization/consumer problems.

Simultaneously, consumers and employees are discovering that using the courts is not a quick and inexpensive path to complaint resolution. Cases often take several years or more to resolve and involve thousands of dollars in expenses. This does not begin to account for human time and energy diverted from other tasks and interests.

This litigation situation raises an obvious question: If we do not use the courts to solve problems, just who and what can we use? One of the most exciting developments in this area is the appearance and growing acceptance of troubleshooters, or employee and customer relations representatives. Troubleshooters (either formally defined or unofficial ones) exist in all organizations. They have various titles: manager of employee relations, patient relations representative, student relations coordinator, customer representative, executive assistant. Some are also labeled ombudsmen.

The formal notion of ombudsman has a long history, first appearing in Swedish government circles in the 1800s (Gellhorn, 1966). Ombudsmen have gained wide acceptance in public administration in this century but have been neglected by the private sector with only brief mention of their potential usefulness (Silver, 1967). Corporate troubleshooters are pervasive but are not identified by any particular title and are not in the private sector literature under the title of ombudsman (Ziegenfuss, 1985c). The use of ombudsmen in organizations generally, and especially in private sector organizations, is a fairly recent development, particularly when the job is labeled and identified as a formal position (Rowe, 1987; Robbins and Deane, 1986). This is underscored by the fact that there are few publications on corporate ombudsmen; the literature in professional business journals is only beginning to emerge (Armstrong, 1983; Clark, 1985). Even so, by now there are many formal ombudsmen at work in the three service fields of government, health, and education. Together, these formally recognized ombudsmen are a large group, though they are only a small part of all troubleshooters at work in organizations across the country (see Chapter Two).

The problem is how to develop greater awareness of the concept of troubleshooting, which is part of the reason I have written this book. There are barriers to this awareness. For example, both public and private organizations are very concerned about their image. They are wary about letting the public hear of their organizational problems. This means that corporations that have begun to use troubleshooters are reluctant to talk about it, even when they have found them to be very effective. This reticence and fear is hampering the diffusion of an innovative, exciting concept. It is unfortunate because it is potentially one of the most productive dispute resolution mechanisms to surface (Robbins and Deane, 1986). Dispute resolution programs and methods are increasingly needed for a wide range of reasons both internal and external to the corporation (McGillis, 1980, 1982). That is, there are external pressures *pushing* as well as internal pressures *pulling* organizations toward troubleshooter program development. A review of some illustrative pressures will demonstrate the intensity of this push and pull.

External Pressures—The Push from Without

Organizations are increasingly being pressured to confront and resolve problems that have only in part been created within the boundaries of the organization. Both public and private organizations exist in a complex organizational environment that includes social, political, and economic influences. A review of some eight environmental areas will begin to map the diversity and depth of this push toward the establishment of troubleshooter programs. These eight external pressure areas are law, economics, culture, technology, education, politics, sociology, and demography (Kast and Rosenzweig, 1985).

A first area of concern for private employers and increasingly for public ones is the threat and the actuality of increased *litigation* from employees. The movement for employees' rights is gaining greater strength each year (Westin and Salisbury, 1980). Clearly the time when corporations could have it entirely their own way is past. The costs of litigation over wrongful termination, sexual harassment, racial discrimination, and frivolous management actions are higher each year. Ewing's book *Do It My Way or You're Fired!* (1983) is a good example of the current concern for the costs of litigation and the changing nature of the organizational response to employee demands.

A second area that frequently leads to conflict with employees is *economic* pressure. Cost control has been a particularly high priority in recent years, as American corporations have been streamlined to compete successfully with foreign companies. Disputes over layoffs, plant closings and relocations, and general concern for productivity have all laid the groundwork for significant conflict between labor and management. Public sector organizations have been experiencing similar conflict during the last five to seven or eight years, in some cases for the first time. Economic pressure due to governmental budget cutbacks and general retrenchment is real and significant. This economic pressure will continue to be there as we move toward the turn of the century, and as long as it exists, mechanisms for solving organizational conflict will need to be developed.

The third external pressure area is *culture*, the goals, values, and other characteristics of the society in which the organizations exist. We have been seeing a general tendency toward assertiveness, toward democratization in the workplace, and toward demands for participation in management and organizational decision making

(Hill, 1971). The expectations of the work force are increasing rapidly. Books such as Jenkins (1974), for example, identify changes that have taken place in the last decade in the values of the people in the labor pool from which the work force is drawn. These changes are setting up conflicts between the newer assertiveness and participative values of the work force on the one hand and the way in which companies have traditionally been organized and managed on the other.

A fourth external pressure area is *technology*. It is news to no one that technological development is proceeding at a rapid pace in practically every field. This has led to both real and hypothesized nightmares about work dislocation and replacement by automation. Workers often experience conflict over the perceived advantages of the new technology and the threat of job change.

A fifth major external pressure that is providing momentum for troubleshooter programs is *education*. The work force in nearly all industries has become better and better educated, and has a different set of interests and values than in earlier years. Employees are able to identify their own needs and interests and are increasingly demanding that they be met. Additionally, an educated work force means fewer employees who are willing to "do it the organization's way" without some opportunity to create new and innovative solutions. In short, the higher level of education leads to conflict between a paternalistic industrial or government culture and a work force that is sophisticated, assertive, and ready to use a variety of skills and abilities.

Sixth, with regard to *politics*, federal, state, and local government is increasingly looking to corporations to provide equity, both in their dealings with employees and as members of the community. That is, government is putting more and more pressure on companies to manage their labor/management relations fairly. The goal is to ensure that both private corporations and government agencies deal responsibly and honestly with employees. For this reason government is increasingly willing to get involved in labor/management disputes and to actively assist in resolving conflicts. A solution would be for corporations to create their own conflict resolution mechanisms that would obviate the necessity for this interference.

There are also *sociological* changes—changes in the way the work force and individual segments of it are organized—that create pressure for troubleshooter programs. For example, employees are increasingly refusing to relocate as quickly as corporations would like them to. Additionally, there is considerably more family/corporation conflict as a result of two-wage earner families attempting to balance the responsibilities of job and home. There are also changing patterns of career development as more and more women become interested in significant career advancement. Women are increasingly willing to confront the "old boy network" that has restricted their advancement in the past. These and other sociological shifts are creating more conflicts between workers and employers. These conflicts can either be resolved by mechanisms within the organization, or they will be made public in the courts.

Finally, there are *demographic* changes that lay the ground-work for increasing stress and conflict in organizations. The most obvious of these is the aging of the work force. As more and more people arrive at age sixty-five able and willing to continue working, how will retirement issues be dealt with and how will job performance issues be managed in a way that is fair from the standpoint of both individual and company? So far, these problems have not been handled very effectively. There are also concerns about the relocation of the work force. For example, if the labor pool declines or if a company desires another location, how can worker/organization relations be maintained?

On a more fundamental level, we might point to developments that cut across all the categories mentioned above. For example, the changes cited by Naisbitt (1982) are contributors to the ferment that produces both complaints and an external push for conflict resolution. Naisbitt identified key trends affecting the depth and pace of change in society some years ago. The list is a lesson in context, the world "out there" to which managers frequently do not relate. His ten trends can be seen as additional potential pressures for troubleshooter programs. He points out (1982) that society is changing

1.   from an industrial society to an information society
2.   from forced technology to hi-tech/hi-touch

3. from a national economy to a world economy
4. from short term to long term
5. from centralization to decentralization
6. from institutional help to self-help
7. from representative democracy to participatory democracy
8. from hierarchies to networking
9. from north to south
10. from either/or to multiple option

How do these trends lead to conflict and a need for trouble-shooters? In general, the trends reflect increasing change within organizations as well as in society as a whole. We are moving from an industrial culture to an information-dominated one. At the same time, we are shifting from a technological imperative to more humanized technology. We are facing the dislocation and competition of a world economy, whereas we had only a national economy in the past. We are forcing people to think about long-term as opposed to short-term commitments, and we are increasingly moving toward decentralization in an attempt to recognize individual autonomy and freedom for personal development. We are learning that institutional help will not solve everything, and that we must solve our own problems; we are also moving from representative democracy to individual involvement at all levels. Information flow hierarchies are no longer as important as they were, since we are increasingly interested in networking. Our orientation is shifting from north to south, and we are looking for multiple options on practically everything.

This tremendous upheaval in society at large exerts considerable pressure on corporations and public agencies to adapt. In the process of adaptation, conflicts between organizations and employees arise on a continual basis. This creates a tremendous need for troubleshooter programs that facilitate individual and organizationwide change.

Internal Pressures—The Pull from Within

Organizations can and must respond to external pressures for change and development. But rarely are these pressures entirely external. The emerging interest in the redesign of public and private organizations (signaled for example by Naisbitt and Aburdene, 1985, and by Ackoff, 1974) means that there are significant internal pressures for change as well. They are derived from beliefs about the nature of organizations themselves as well as from more specific assumptions about the characteristics of public and private organizations.

Do employees complain? Do consumers complain? The answer is obviously yes to both questions. Employee complaints are commonplace in all organizations, both public and private. That fact is a given about the nature of the organizational world! Some employees change jobs because of an inability to tolerate general corporate or specific management conditions, only to find that similar problems exist in the new organization. The search for a complaint-free organization is a futile one. The real question is, how does your organization handle complaints? Are they ignored, or are they acknowledged and responded to? The second alternative—acknowledgment and resolution by troubleshooters—is the result of a *pull from within* organizations, a pull that involves a convergence of different trends.

First, it is rapidly becoming known that "good" organizations (that is, those with high productivity *and* positive working conditions) devote a large amount of time and energy to listening to their employees and customers. Peters and Waterman's book *In Search of Excellence* (1984) reinforced and broadened our recognition of this. Productive service organizations like hospitals and highly regarded corporations such as IBM use listening as a way to learn about organizational successes *and* failures—what they are doing well and what needs to be improved. Without actual data, they feel they are not well enough informed to take appropriate actions.

Second, part of this rationale for listening is the realization that it has payoffs for the "bottom line." Quite simply, organizations want to do more of what they do well and eliminate what they are not doing well, since the latter results in lost time, energy, and money, regardless of whether they are manufacturing toasters or are providing patient care. In short, if management listens well, an organization will perform better.

Third, listening is a part of a more general movement toward participative management. This management approach is based on the belief that the more employees participate, the stronger the organization will be. With greater participation, management is better able to respond to the complexity of the world and to the demands of the employees, customers, and suppliers who have a stake in the organization. Complaining is one way that these individuals can participate. Management responses tell them whether their participation is effective in generating action—in other words, whether their views and needs "count for anything."

The participative movement is also derived in part from a more negative trend. The fourth trend is the dramatic increase in litigation by employees. This was cited as an external pressure, but it is reiterated here as internally derived as well. Both private corporations and public agencies are increasingly being sued for a wide variety of reasons ranging from unjust firing to discrimination. In many cases, these are unresolved complaints, many of which could have been addressed without the use of the courts (for example, through the redesign of policies and procedures; Lublin, 1983). Because organizations are often not responsive or at least do not seem to be responsive, both customers and employees sue. Actual litigation, the threat of litigation, and a desire for prevention therefore constitute a powerful "internal pull."

Litigation is also part of a fifth and larger trend, the employee rights movement. Labor unions protect the constitutional rights of workers in large organizations. In smaller and nonunion organizations there are wide variations with regard to privacy, dissent, and due process in work-related issues. Considerations relating to the quality of working life dictate that the protection of constitutional rights is essential to worker satisfaction. Employees are increasingly demanding fair treatment. Complaints are often just the start of this process, which ends in litigation when the complaints are ignored.

So far, the trends cited have been employee-oriented. But customers complain as well. The sixth trend is the renewed attention to customer relations. A somewhat novel idea—that customers *should* complain and that the organization *should* listen—is now recognized as critical to productivity and to the maintenance of quality. This is because customer complaints increase productivity by bringing problems to light that are indicators of quality gaps. In other words, they enhance quality by flagging deficient goods and services for attention by management and technical personnel.

The seventh trend involves the development and testing of alternative dispute resolution methods. Alternatives to the human and financial costs of litigation (including lowered profits and poor quality of working life) are in great demand. The problems are not new ones, but to a great extent the solutions are still not apparent. Some new methods are beginning to be recognized for their successes, though. This book is of course devoted to highlighting one response to this search for faster and more effective means of dispute resolution.

The eighth trend that is part of the internal pull toward troubleshooter programs is the desire to create open communication. Many of those who find fault with management focus on communication problems as a key source of difficulty in troubled organizations. Therefore, an interest in developing more open communication between employees and management is leading the list of development tasks for contemporary managers. A completely open communication system is one that includes opportunities for employees and customers to complain freely and responsibly about difficulties in the workplace or with the goods and services provided by the company. A troubleshooter is one more means by which employees and consumers can exercise this communication function. Some critics suggest that troubleshooters are actually interfering with the process of communication by allowing employees or customers to circumvent division directors or vice presidents. However, this reflects views about the way the world should be, not how it actually is! We all know of managers who are difficult to talk to. The fact that an alternative communication channel exists is a positive force in a complex organization.

The ninth trend is a desire to reduce turnover, for example, in many hi-tech industries and in specific job classes where turnover is high, such as in nursing positions in hospitals. As an illustration, in several major Fortune 500 companies, troubleshooters consider one of their most significant benefits to be the reduction of turnover among highly paid scientists and technical personnel. The problem is, of course, that employees with complaints usually make a few attempts to have them addressed, and when this does not happen, they begin to look for other jobs.

The tenth trend is somewhat philosophical, and involves efforts to create justice and equity within organizations. Does a sense of fairness prevail? Has the corporation or public agency done all it can to promote justice among both employees and consumers? Ethical problems and the lack of fair treatment at the hands of managers and employees have caused much grief to workers and customers alike. As we will see, troubleshooter programs are one of the more important methods by which justice and fairness can be promoted within organizations.

The eleventh trend is an overall interest in humanizing the organization. As Naisbitt's comments about the increasing trend toward hi-tech and hi-touch revealed, we are trying to humanize modern technology, by reducing its more impersonal or destructive aspects. The continuing development of technology is not rejected; it is only tempered by a concern for social and psychological needs. One way to do this is to create positions with the responsibility to address human concerns—both the actual wrongs experienced by workers and consumers and the perceived ones (which are frequently as damaging) (Hogan, 1980).

The twelfth trend is an interest in developing a corporate culture that represents values and goals that are attractive to both managers and employees. These values and goals include an emphasis on openness and participation and on a problem-solving approach that says that the complaints of all employees and customers are valued, whether the setting is a university, a major corporation, a hospital, or a prison. The presence of troubleshooters is both a symbolic and an actual reflection of a cultural value of openness and a willingness to listen. This is a very powerful pull that is just now beginning to exert an influence as more recognition is given to the notion of organizational culture.

The final trend that contributes to an internal pull is the success of troubleshooter programs in those organizations that have tried them. Typically, these programs have initially met with some resistance; once underway, though, they tend to be highly valued by managers and employees as well as by customers. Moreover, the solution of problem after problem by expert troubleshooters is a strong recommendation for the development of troubleshooter programs in other companies in the same industries and for an expansion across fields. This is in part why more and more programs are being established in industry, education, health care, corrections, and elsewhere. It is obvious, in short, that the idea is not gaining acceptance because of failure, but instead because of success.

Summary

This first chapter has attempted to identify some of the pressures that are leading to the development of troubleshooter programs in various industries. We have not made an attempt here to systematically track the history of troubleshooter programs in business, education, health care, corrections, and other fields, since this has been done elsewhere (Ziegenfuss, 1985c). However, illuminating the overall trends that are leading corporate executives in the troubleshooter direction is important.

Most managers will recognize the trends outlined above. They were described as creating either a *push* or a *pull*, the push being external pressures coming primarily from outside the organization and the pull, forces within the organization that are providing momentum for troubleshooter programs. The external pressures were categorized in terms of law, economics, culture, technology, education, politics, sociology, and demography; the internal pressures were identified as a desire for excellence and productivity as well as for more organizational learning, more participative management, less employee litigation, more secure employee rights, better customer relations, dispute resolution methods that improve the quality of working life, open communication, reduced employee turnover, greater justice and equity, more humane organizations, a more democratic corporate culture, and the emulation of the successes of early troubleshooter programs. These trends are now spreading to many new industries, both here and abroad, and so it is not surprising that more and more troubleshooter programs are appearing. In the next chapter, the troubleshooter concept is introduced in greater detail.

2

Different Methods
for Solving Problems

Why Handle Complaints?

Complaint programs, including those using troubleshooters, are designed to

- promote excellence
- increase organizational learning
- increase participation
- decrease litigation
- promote positive customer and employee relations

Productive, quality-oriented organizations *listen* to employees and customers using complaints to help change (that is, improve) the organization. This statement holds for both private and public organizations, including industries as diverse as manufacturing and health care. For example, Rowe (1987, p. 133) noted that

> CEOs who have added an ombuds office usually justify its creation by one or more of these three statements:
>
> - the office more than pays for itself—it is cost-effective;
> - the rights and responsibilities of employees and of the company are well supported by such an office;
> - it is humane and caring human resource policy to have such an office.

Ombudsmen in corporations exist because CEOs see cost benefits, believe in employee rights and responsibilities, and feel that the program is part of a good human resources policy. Similar concerns apply in the area of health care, where patient representatives or troubleshooters handle complaints that target staff behavior, medical and nursing care, environmental comfort, admissions, bills, and follow-up care—a full range of "customer" concerns. Hospital and nursing home troubleshooters help to ensure that quality is maintained and that problems are quickly and effectively addressed. The presence of troubleshooters gives comfort to friends and relatives of patients and to patients themselves because "someone" has the responsibility for attacking problems. There are now approximately 3,000 patient representatives (or health care troubleshooters) in hospitals across the country (American Hospital Association, personal communication, Dec. 1987).

A General Definition of Troubleshooters

The Oxford American Dictionary defines a troubleshooter as "a person employed to trace and correct faults in machinery, etc., or to act as a mediator in disputes." Today these individuals provide general problem solving. The problems they handle for fellow employees range from hiring, firing, and promotion conflicts to sexual harassment cases. Troubleshooters for customers—patient representatives, customer relations representatives, consumer advocates—address such issues as product quality and product deficiency, support/repair service needs, billing and payment, organization responsiveness, and general satisfaction. Other concerns that receive their attention can be inferred from the fact that there are currently troubleshooters (who have many different job titles) in the following organizations: hospitals; nursing homes; the military; defense contractors; manufacturing companies; educational institutions, including both colleges and school districts; correctional institutions; federal, state, and local government; public utilities; banks; churches; journalism; and television and radio stations. (According to recent articles in *Time* (Dec. 7, 1981, p. 62) and *Business Week* (Feb. 12, 1979, p. 117), specific corporations that have complaint-processing mechanisms include

IBM, American Express, TWA, Tektronix, Chemical Bank, Citibank, McDonald's, Singer, Northrop, Florida Power and Light, and others. Their programs differ significantly, of course, and range from a "people-intensive personal problem-solving system" to correspondence and telephone-based systems. Some are formally recognized programs with staff and support services, while others involve only a single individual handling complaints.) Trouble-shooters may have a wide range of job titles; the following list is certainly not exhaustive: employee relations manager, counselor, corporate ombudsman, equal employment opportunity specialist, human relations specialist, employee communications director, public relations specialist, employee representative, human resources director. [One of the first surveys of members of the Corporate Ombudsman Association revealed that specific titles include Alternative Communications Channel; Assistant to Secretary for Citizen Affairs; Corporate Ombudsman; Employee Problem Resolution Officer; Exempt Compensation Program Manager; Franchise Liaison Manager; Manager, Employee Relations; Manager, Human Resources; Manager, Work Problems Counseling; Ombuds Assistant; Principal Staff Engineer—Ombudsman; Special Assistant to CEO; Vice President; Vice President—Ombudsman; Ombudsman and Ombudsperson (Ziegenfuss, Robbins, and Rowe, 1987, p. 38).]

The range of titles indicates that no consensus has been reached yet on a main troubleshooter label, or for that matter on the functions of these individuals. Nevertheless, the characteristics of troubleshooters can be summarized as follows. Troubleshooters

- focus on communication and active listening
- use a wide variety of techniques from coaching to confrontation
- serve in virtually all industries
- distribute their work time among complaint handling, education, and consultation activities
- rely on personal charisma as well as organizational position
- come from a wide variety of educational backgrounds
- are paid from $25,000 in health care to $100,000+ in private industry (Ziegenfuss, Robbins, and Rowe, 1987)

Formal and Informal Troubleshooters Defined

As we noted earlier, there are two types of troubleshooters, formal ones and informal ones. The second group vastly outnumbers the first. Formal troubleshooting functions are particularly common in jobs with titles like customer relations representative, manager of employee relations, human relations director, executive assistant, human resources director, and corporate ombudsman. Informal troubleshooters fulfill this role in addition to their normal responsibilities. (Figure 1 indicates the relationship between formal troubleshooters such as employee and customer representatives and the large group of informal problem solvers.)

Figure 1. Troubleshooters: Formal and Informal (Formal Troubleshooters Are Denoted by the Shaded Area).

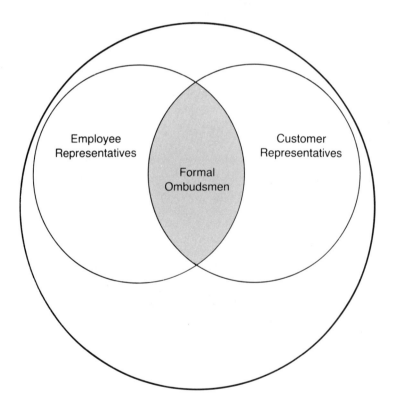

Figure 2. Troubleshooters: Tree Diagram.

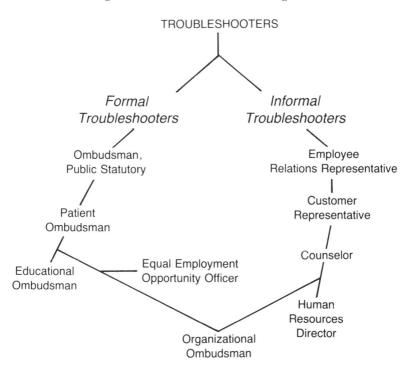

To think of troubleshooters in formal versus informal terms is to think of them as branches of a tree, as shown in Figure 2. Both formal and informal troubleshooter types belong to the same family, though clearly to separate branches. The first group is formally recognized and funded and may have authority based in law. The informal branch just carries out these functions without official authority and in addition to other duties. It is important to note that the two models can coexist in the same organization, so that for instance a hospital can have both a formal patient representative and an informal employee troubleshooter (such as an employee relations manager who defines his or her job in this way). The point is that there are more similarities than differences in the family; in order to understand this, however, we need to have a more complete understanding of who troubleshooters are and what they do.

Formal troubleshooters are called ombudsmen in the professional and academic literature. The term *ombudsman* has a long and rich history, much of which is associated with the public sector:

> The ombudsman is not a term coined by modern techno-
> logical society for some new invention like radar, micro-
> wave, and transistor. It is an old Swedish word that has
> been used for centuries to describe a person who represents
> or protects the interests of another. It gained a more spe-
> cific meaning in 1809 when the Swedish government ap-
> pointed a public official to investigate public complaints
> against public administration. As the word became more
> frequently used, especially outside Sweden, it was misused
> and corrupted, and it is now often used loosely for any
> public complaints officer, that is, for any officer or office of
> any organization that receives public complaints about the
> way it conducts its business or how others conduct their
> business. Thus, radio stations, newspapers, churches, busi-
> nesses, and other nongovernmental bodies have their own
> ombudsman offices, and it is difficult for people to distin-
> guish the more specific use of the term to refer to govern-
> ment ombudsman offices established to receive complaints
> from the public about the administrative actions of public
> authorities [Caiden, MacDermot, and Sandler, 1983, p. 3].

One of the earliest mentions of the notion of *corporate* ombudsman comes from Silver in a 1967 *Harvard Business Review* article. Silver (1967, p. 77) saw the derivation of the ombudsman concept as based on the notion of corporate social responsibility and fair play. In his view, the ombudsman would be an investigator, a policy interpre-ter, a decision recommender, and a complaint denier (for inappro-priate complaints). Only two groups would be excluded from using the ombudsman—top management and unionized personnel. (Other historical information on the ombudsman concept is provided by Gellhorn, 1966; Ziegenfuss, 1985c; Rowat, 1964; Reuss and Anderson, 1966; Capozzola, 1968; Verkuil, 1975; Foegen, 1972; Gwyn, 1975; Pugh, 1978.)

How can we describe the purposes and activities of ombuds-men? The organizers of the first Corporate Ombudsman Conference were faced with exactly this task, and decided on a definition of ombudsman that would include a wider range of organizational problem solvers than it excluded: "Ombudsman—one skilled in dealing with reported complaints to help achieve equitable settlements" (Corporate Ombudsman Association, 1984). In other words, their job is to take complaints, investigate conflicts, and help to create solutions to problems. Some examples may help to make this clear.

A newspaper report provided the following account of a corporate ombudsman program:

> United Technologies Corp. established a corporate ombudsman program last summer. It went into effect in August. Overseeing the program is Walter F. Eells, vice president and ombudsman.
>
> The program is designed to enable confidential communication in writing or through a toll-free phone service between employees and top officials of the corporation and its operating units.
>
> Eells, who joined the company in 1956, most recently was vice president for management development and salaried personnel relations at UTC. He previously served in a variety of personnel assignments at other company units including Pratt & Whitney, Hamilton Standard, Norden Systems and Essex. . . .
>
> Q. How did the program come about?
>
> A. Back in early April we decided we wanted to have a two-way employee communication system of the broadest possible kind. So top management asked the corporate human resource staff to look at what's being done around the country and make a recommendation on what action UTC might take. I was assigned the responsibility to do that study. We implemented the written, confidential two-way communication program (DIALOG) on August 1 [Ross, 1986, p. 6].

The purpose here was to encourage and provide the means for employee communication. Employees are just one troubleshooter client group, however. A patient ombudsman in a hospital has a formal role that involves listening to patients' complaints about treatment and support services:

In tears, the young woman entered Patricia
O'Rourke's office at the Royal Victoria Hospital.

As patient representative, O'Rourke's job is to sort
out the problems and complaints of the hospital's patients
and their families, and she encouraged her visitor to un-
burden herself.

"She was from a rural community and had just been
told by her surgeon that she required an operation that was
not lifesaving, but ultimately necessary," O'Rourke said.

"The surgeon saw no reason to wait and had already
booked the operating room for two days later. He urged her
to make a decision that day."

But the patient was feeling pressured and upset. She
told O'Rourke she didn't understand what the operation
really involved and she wanted to go home and discuss it
with her family.

"That seemed quite reasonable to me," O'Rourke
said. "But she was worried that she would offend the surgeon if she refused her immediate consent. I told her it was
her body and her hesitation was quite normal."

O'Rourke immediately arranged for a nurse to outline the operation to the patient. Then she put in a call to
the surgeon to explain the woman's hesitation and to make
sure the operation could be safely delayed, which he
confirmed.

"The upshot was the patient went home, discussed
the operation with her family and returned confidently for
the operation three months later."

O'Rourke functions as an ombudsman, a position
that is gradually becoming more common in Canadian institutions and corporations [Carson, 1986, p. F-1].

This story illustrates both the purpose and a possible outcome of ombudsman programs in hospitals—greater peace of mind
for the patient.

On the informal side, some clients of agencies become
troubleshooters for colleagues. The following account identifies an
informal but highly visible troubleshooter for a county welfare
agency.

Every prison has its jailhouse lawyer.

The Dauphin County Assistance Office has Robert
Richardson.

> Richardson, 57, of Hall Manor is a welfare recipient.
> Yet, every weekday from 9 A.M. to 2 P.M., he is at the wel-
> fare office at 124 Pine St., giving advice.
>
> Often clad in a suit, tie and tennis shoes, Richardson
> sits at a table in a corner with his briefcase. Near him is a
> handmade sign taped to the wall, which says, "Contact Mr.
> Richardson for your welfare problems."
>
> He said he is there because of "a dedication to help
> the ones who need help."
>
> He also says:
>
> "I'm like an advocate who represents all clients from
> Dauphin County.
>
> "I'm kind of a troubleshooter. I try to straighten out
> problems."
>
> Unlike some welfare advocates, Richardson gets
> along with the assistance office management.
>
> "He has been a great help to us. I think people feel
> more free to talk to him because he has no ax to grind,"
> said James Hindinger, executive director of the local office.
>
> "I have a rapport with Mr. Hindinger and the
> workers," Richardson said. "He appreciates the work I am
> doing as a liaison between the caseworker and the recip-
> ient" (*Harrisburg Patriot News*, 1986).

As we have seen, the welfare troubleshooter is at the informal end of the continuum, a continuum that includes everything from volunteers to those with fully recognized authority. Despite this diversity, though, troubleshooters tend to deal with certain basic kinds of problems.

Types of Complaints Handled

The extent of troubleshooting activity in a wide variety of industries from manufacturing to health care suggests that complaint topics are almost limitless. As we stated earlier, examples drawn from the business sphere may include personnel policies, physical conditions, recreational activities, sexual harassment, discrimination, supervisory conflict, interdepartmental conflict, production processes, personality conflict, personal problems, and general dispute resolution. A formal troubleshooter (ombudsman) could cite the following cases from a typical month of employee complaints:

- A manager asked the ombudsman confidentially to find out where he stands. Through an organizational change, he had lost some of his responsibilities. Finding: He was still very highly regarded. The change was made to prepare for an anticipated work load increase in the area he retained.
- A complaint about "forced" overtime among engineers. Finding: The company policy was fair and correct, but some managers were operating by their own interpretations, which were not always correct. A frank letter from the vice president helped, but it did not entirely eliminate these abuses.
- The denial of medical insurance payments to an employee for reasons unclear to him. Finding: The claim was payable and the man got his money.

A patient ombudsman in a hospital had these sample patient (customer) complaints:

- inadequate information from a physician about an upcoming surgical procedure
- an incorrect bill that was seemingly inexplicable
- "missing civility" toward an elderly grandmother from the floor's night nursing team
- stolen watch and ring from the bedside

In each of these instances, the troubleshooter action involved investigation, communication with the involved parties, and follow-up. These may not be the types of complaints handled in all systems, but they are representative. For customers, the complaints are very wide ranging, involving such items as product quality and service, sales practices, return policy, and billing. In spite of this obvious diversity, though, the complaints tend to share some common features. More specifically, they are of an interpersonal rather than a technical nature for the most part, or at least involve personal judgments. As an illustration, consider the following two cases.

Data Fudging

Deborah Thornton was a young and dedicated scientist in an industrial research and development laboratory. She was working as a part of a new-product team that was developing a new artificial sweetener. One afternoon, she noticed a discrepancy in one senior scientist's reports and checked it. It appeared he was "fudging" the data but she was not sure. He was an irascible guy. Since he would be responsible for her promotions and her continued work on the project, she was afraid to ask him about it. She did not want to embarrass or anger him and had no idea what to do, so she just watched and worried, becoming more and more distracted.

Privacy Violation

Walter Matthews was a senior engineer in a major paper company. At age forty-seven, he had spent twenty-seven years working at that company. He contracted cancer and needed treatment, but he was determined to carry on as before. He was shocked to find an announcement of his medical condition posted on the bulletin board. Tearing it down, he went to the department supervisor to complain and to request privacy. The supervisor was unsympathetic and refused to have his name removed from the illness list.

Though most programs consider *no* complaints to be insignificant, there is some natural sorting out as larger problems displace smaller ones in priority. For example, a complaint about inadequate lighting is important but is less immediately demanding of attention than potential sabotage, suicide, or sexual harassment. The next question that will concern us is what do troubleshooters do with these complaints when they get them?

Primary Troubleshooter Activities

In my own research (Ziegenfuss, 1985c) and through the troubleshooter programs I have helped to design and develop (Ziegenfuss, Charette, and Guenin, 1984), I have come to the conclusion that troubleshooting involves three primary activities: complaint processing, education and training, and consultation. This is not a perfect classification since the categories overlap, but the commonly accepted definitions of these activities describe reasonably well what troubleshooters do. Complaint processing includes fact finding through investigation, feedback of the data to the participants, and problem/conflict resolution. Education involves teaching organizational members, for example, about company or agency policies, procedures, and the rationale for decisions. Consultation is advisory work with senior and middle management regarding both problems and proposed actions for resolution and for prevention.

In a description of troubleshooter activities, Rowe (1987, pp. 130–131) identified eight principal functions pertaining to corporate ombudsmen but certainly relevant to troubleshooters in general. These amount to a definition of troubleshooter activities:

1. *Dealing with Feelings*
   On occasion, living and working bring rage, grief and bewilderment to everyone. Managers and employees often feel there has been "no one to listen." Possibly the most important function of a complaint handler (or complaint system) is to deal with feelings. If this function is not otherwise provided, by line and staff managers, it will fall to the ombudsman . . . .

2. *Giving and Receiving Information on a One-to-One Basis*
   Many employees do not even know the name of their CEO, much less how the company determines promotions, transfers, or benefits, or how it deals with problems in the work place like harassment. It is therefore very important that line and staff managers be prepared to give out information, and make referrals to helping resources, on a one-to-one basis, at the time and in the fashion needed by an individual with a problem. This may again be all that is needed. If appropriate information and referrals are not made available by other managers, this function may fall to the ombudsman . . . .

3. *Counseling and Problem-Solving to Help the Manager or Employee Help Himself or Herself*
   Many employees and managers face tenacious problems with only three alternatives in mind: to quit, to put up with their problem, or to start some formal process of complaint, or suit or investigation.

   These are not the only alternatives, nor are they always the best available. The skilled ombudsman will help a visitor develop and explore and role-play new

options, then help the visitor choose an option, then
follow-up to see that it worked. And in many cases, the
best option may be for the person with a problem to
seek to deal with it effectively on his or her own . . . .

4. *Shuttle Diplomacy*
Sometimes a visitor will opt for a go-between. This is
especially true where one or more parties need to save
face or deal with emotions before a good solution can
be found. This is much the most common type of intervention reported by ombuds practitioners, especially
if the company is quite hierarchical in style and organization. In some companies, this function may also be
pursued by the ombudsman—during or between the
steps of a formal, complaint-and-appeal grievance process—as an option for settling outside any adjudicatory
process.

5. *Mediation*
At other times, a visitor will choose the option of meeting *with* others, together with the ombudsman. Like
shuttle diplomacy, this usually happens on an informal basis. However, the "settlements" of shuttle diplomacy and mediation may be made formal by the
parties involved.

6. *Investigation*
Investigation of a problem or a complaint can be formal or informal, with or without recommendations to
an adjudicator—for example, to a grievance committee
or to a line or senior manager. All four of these investi-
gatory options are reported by ombuds practitioners,
and are more or less common depending on the company and the ombudsman.

7. *Adjudication or Arbitration*
This function is very rare for the ombudsman. Here,
the classic phrase about ombuds practitioners is likely
to obtain: "They may not make or change or set aside
a management rule or decision: theirs is the power of
reason and persuasion."

8. *Upward Feedback*
Possibly the most important function of the ombudsman is to receive, perhaps analyze, then pass along information that will foster timely change in a company.
Where policies are outdated or unintelligible, or new
problems have arisen, or a new diversity appears in the
employee pool, an ombudsman may be a low-key,

steady-state change agent at very low cost to the
employer.

> This function also provides a mechanism for
> dealing with some very difficult confidentiality prob-
> lems. An ombudsman can, for example, suggest that a
> department head instigate an apparently "routine"
> department-wide discussion about safety or harassment
> or waste-management or theft, in response to an indi-
> vidual concern, at no cost to anyone's privacy or
> rights, in such a way as to eliminate an individual
> problem (if not necessarily the perpetrator).

Individually and collectively, these activities are the ones that lead
to the realization of the goals presented at the outset of Chapter
One. To shed further light on troubleshooting, we must explore the
primary activity of complaint processing.

The individual methods of complaint taking used by
troubleshooters vary, but there seem to be five steps that are central
to this process. These were distilled from a review of work in many
industries (Ziegenfuss, 1985c). Though not all troubleshooters
follow these steps in each case, they are generally representative of
the nature of complaint-handling work.

> *Step 1:* *Identify the Complaint.* This initial step involves
> reviewing the general problem as to facts and
> context, then reducing the complaint to a specific
> one-sentence problem (often not as easy as it would
> appear). Once the primary problem is identified,
> troubleshooters define the secondary problems if
> any.
>
> *Step 2:* *Investigate the Complaint.* Troubleshooters outline
> a procedure for investigation and further clarify the
> problem, if necessary. They then follow the usual
> procedure for investigation and discuss the facts
> and context of the case and create relevant and
> specific recommendations. Recommendations for
> action are then identified.
>
> *Step 3:* *Report the Investigation Results.* In step 3, trouble-
> shooters examine the participants' responses for

agreement, disagreement, or apathy, tailoring actions to participants' positions. Typically, they will write a report (although some do not) and/or hold a face-to-face review.

Step 4: *Develop Responses to the Problems.* Troubleshooters create and spur responses by listening and reflecting, collaborating on the creation of solutions, and independently suggesting alternatives.

Step 5: *Monitor the Response Plans to Ensure Follow-Through.* Troubleshooters examine multiple systems changes according to their proposed time schedule, monitoring solutions effected at both the individual case level (treating problems) and throughout the organization (taking preventive actions).

These troubleshooting steps are generally the same for all types of complaints. Not all steps are taken in each complaint case, though, since the work is actually very fluid and some problems are solved quickly, almost on the spot. For example, many ombudsmen refer complainants with an alcohol or drug problem to an employee assistance program. These cases require little in the way of monitoring for follow-through (step 5); it is only necessary to ensure that contact was made. Other problems call for managers and/or employees to make major changes in personal or organizational behavior that (1) they do not want to make, and/or that (2) require rather extensive periods to complete, such as cases of interpersonal conflict between managers in one department. In other cases, troubleshooters may invest much time in helping the participants create solutions to the problem. All other steps would be minimized in relation to this undertaking.

Obviously some investigations uncover problems that are clear and easily solved, and others yield ambiguity, policy conflict, and much uncertainty about the correct response. Two examples will illustrate this point. The first case exhibits a set of troubleshooter actions drawn from a national survey of corporate ombudsmen (Ziegenfuss, Robbins, and Rowe, 1987). The survey asked ombudsmen to identify which of the following approaches and techniques were used and how often: dealing with feelings, active listening, describing options, giving advice, referral, coaching, shuttle diplomacy, mediation, investigation, making recommendations, turning the case over, arbitration/adjudication, generic intervention, and upward feedback. The first case shows how one ombudsman employed the various techniques.

Case 1: Personal and Organizational Danger

In a relatively small percentage of cases, troubleshooters confront problems that present the potential for serious personal and organizational consquences. Case 1 illustrates this.

    The Complaint The employee presenting the complaint was an engineer in a research and development unit of a major defense contractor. Age forty-eight, he had worked for the company for some nineteen years as a loyal and solid performer. For the last two years, he had been technical engineering chief on a weapons system research and development project. His project involved competing with another project group to complete a design task increasing traction on a new-model army tank. The competition was intense and involved major bonuses and promotions. Both project groups depended on a joint supply stream for materials for their prototypes. Unfortunately, the engineer's project manager and the supply manager were fighting through an intense personality conflict.

    When supplies became limited, the supply chief directed the scarce supplies to the other project team (partly in spite). When the engineer confronted the supply chief, his own project director would not back him up. Since this would mean they would lose the competition (started thirty-six months ago), he was outraged. After two sleepless nights, he went to the corporate ombudsman.

    Ombudsmen Activities The engineer appeared obviously distraught and looked like he had not been sleeping. He told his story with clear and significant anger. The ombudsman began with *active listening*, helping him to specify the problem as completely as he could. Along with listening, the ombudsman expressed sympathy and extended understanding of his concern and disappointment (*dealing with feelings*). He asked the engineer what action he was contemplating. The engineer suggested only half-jokingly that he would kill himself or wipe out the project (sabotage?).

He told the engineer that he would *investigate* the situation and asked permission to contact the principals. This was okayed by the engineer. They agreed to meet again the next day.

The ombudsman *investigated,* finding the situation to be true, but that there was a possibility of additional supplies if the engineer's manager and the supply chief could come to terms. The ombudsman met again with the engineer, who was still very upset. The ombudsman *described the options*—to move on to a new project or to try to negotiate a treaty. The engineer only reluctantly agreed and was still obviously angry and upset. The ombudsman suggested he meet with a counselor friend to deal with his feelings about the conflict (*referral*).

The next day, the ombudsman initiated *shuttle diplomacy* between the project manager and the supply chief to get them to agree to a meeting and a compromise. Eventually (after two individual visits each), they did meet. Agreement to provide supplies was secured but the conflict was far from over.

The engineer was informed of the resolution but both he and the ombudsman agreed to meet again.

The ombudsman also met with the Division General Manager to inform him of some of the problems emerging in the push for product innovation (*upward feedback*). The ombudsman recommended initiating a series of meet-and-discuss conferences to review the stress and performance situation (*recommendation*). He offered to facilitate if needed.

In this case, the troubleshooter employed a variety of approaches and techniques. The use of many tools in a single case is typical, particularly when outcomes are potentially very severe—suicide and sabotage. This is an apparently serious case. Other cases are serious but do not always appear to be so.

A second case indicates "hidden significance" in a seemingly trivial case involving corporate sports.

Case 2: The Company Softball Game

The Complaint   In one corporation, several employees were heard to complain that the softball umpires had been asked to favor one division's team over the others (Ziegenfuss, 1985b). Divisional business competition was at a high level and it carried over into sports activities. The corporation's official troubleshooter (called a corporate ombudsman) was presented with the complaint after two employees decided it was too "risky" to bring the problem up directly with their divisional boss.

Troubleshooter Actions   The ombudsman began by collecting specifics about the complaint. How was the one team favored by the umpires—calling strikes and balls, close calls on the baselines, and so on? Which umpires were involved? What were the days and specific examples? Who could corroborate the statements? A secondary problem was identified relating to the negative aspects of the intensity of the competition. This was noted but was not the specific subject of the complaint.

The facts were gathered by talking to the umpires, players, and divisional managers. The allegation was found to be true, but it applied only to the last game played. The ombudsman asked for suggestions on how to resolve it. There was rather quick agreement on a replay of the game, with a consensus that the reasons should be deemphasized. The ombudsman suggested a meeting of the two teams to clarify the problem and to diminish the emotional level, particularly the most heated aspects of the competition. The question of whether this was a common problem in other sports activities was raised. The recreation department decided to address the "level of competition" problem in a series of light memos and team discussions. Subsequent softball games and other activities were monitored over the next three months. Though there are complaints that are more serious than this—sabotage, discrimination, and dangerous physical conditions—sports activities are an important part of the corporate culture that must be maintained effectively, without destructive levels of competition.

Summary

We have just considered why complaints are taken seriously by the organization, who is doing complaint processing, and how these individuals work. In bringing this chapter to a close, we should reiterate what the presence of complaint processing means for public and private corporate cultures, a topic that is currently of great interest. With a troubleshooting program in existence, the organizational culture (whether of a manufacturing firm or government agency) has evidence that the welfare of employees and customers is taken seriously, and that sincere efforts will be made to redress any problems that might arise. For this and other reasons, there is little doubt that more private corporations and public agencies will vigorously embrace the troubleshooting concept.

3

The Work of a Troubleshooter

We now have a view of troubleshooting as a whole, but we need to know more about the specifics of the job. This is a harder task than it may appear, since it can be approached in various ways. One alternative is to describe in formal terms what the rules and functions of the job are. Another possibility is to sketch what happens in practical terms—that is, to present an average "day in the life" of a troubleshooter. Both approaches have their advantages, and so I will utilize both of them, beginning with a relatively formal description of troubleshooting activities.

Three Essential Activities

It is useful to begin our discussion of troubleshooting functions with the following case study:

Fired for Refusing Unethical Practice

A department store clerk was told by her supervisor to inform customers that there were only six of the special sale AM-FM radios at $19.99. A similar model was available for $29.95 of which plenty were on hand. When a customer came in after the last of the six $19.95 radios were sold asking for one, the clerk checked the inventory. She found there were plenty of less expensive radios and informed her supervisor that she would not lie to customers. He told her that there were great financial rewards involved in staying with current sales policy and that he was offered these rewards. They were attractive to him—he said he was "on board." She refused and was promptly fired for insubordination.

If the department store clerk wanted to complain about being fired, who would she talk to and what would happen? A complaint to the supervisor who fired her would not accomplish much. Personnel could listen, but the complainant would fear bias. A complaint to a troubleshooter—the employee relations manager, an executive assistant friend, or a formal corporate ombudsman—would generate a fair hearing and relevant action. The question, of course, is what exactly would a troubleshooter do?

We saw in the previous chapter that troubleshooting involves three primary activities (complaint processing, education and training, and consultation) and that complaint processing is the most important of these. This central function in turn involves

- taking complaints
- gathering the facts through investigation
- reporting on their conclusions
- suggesting follow-up actions
- monitoring to see that those actions are taking place

With regard to our opening case, a troubleshooter would process the clerk's complaint by gathering the facts, reporting to management, and helping to identify a solution(s).

Second, troubleshooters are educators and trainers for the corporation or public agency. Policies, procedures, and other organizational rules and regulations need to be transmitted to employees. Troubleshooting programs provide one way of educating and training employees regarding the full range of organizational purposes, policies, and rules. This education occurs in both formal and informal sessions, and for example may include small workshops and informal employee visits. The department store clerk's supervisor attempted to "educate" the clerk about the degree of fit between her view and his view of the corporation's policies. The troubleshooter and other corporate executives may need to reeducate the supervisor about corporate values and sales policies.

Last, troubleshooters act as consultants to management, employees, and customers, helping them solve a wide range of problems. Public agencies are quite accustomed to the idea that independent troubleshooters such as ombudsmen can be helpful to government by diagnosing and presenting problems (see Gellhorn, 1966; Caiden, 1983). Private corporations are increasingly recognizing the usefulness of troubleshooters as internal consultants for developmental help and for impartial refereeing (Rowe, 1987; Robbins and Deane, 1986). Someone will need to referee the conflict between the supervisor and the clerk. If clear policies are violated by the firing, other action will need to be taken. If this is "accepted organizational behavior," some feedback to management about potential negative consequences is warranted. A troubleshooter as consultant can provide this feedback to the CEO in a way that maximizes the chance of constructive use of the information.

This is a good starting description of the troubleshooter's job. In the following pages, we elaborate on this description, and also discuss a few other issues related to troubleshooting activities.

Complaint Processing

We now need to consider the more specific actions involved in complaint processing. What steps should be taken by the troubleshooter when the department store clerk presents her complaint? The actions that we will discuss are not limited to the department store situation, but apply to troubleshooters as they process a wide range of other complaints—for example, from patients in hospitals, employees in scientific labs, and students and faculty in colleges and universities.

One view of the functions of a troubleshooter comes from an article by Rowe and Baker (1984). They identify five interrelated functions that they feel the troubleshooter or ombudsman provides:

- personal communication
- confidential advice and counseling
- investigation, conciliation, and mediation
- adjudication
- upward feedback

Surveying all of these functions and providing examples will extend our definition of the troubleshooter's job. (As you read the descriptions, it will be helpful to keep the diagram in Figure 3 in mind.) Each function is a contributor to the whole and each interacts with the other functions. For example, investigation of the store clerk's problem is not just an independent part of the troubleshooter's job but an interconnected part that will also involve personal communication and upward feedback to the CEO about corporate values and professional ethics. Each function relates to all of the others and to the whole task of complaint handling. This somewhat abstract idea will be evident in the descriptions of the various functions.

Communication   Many corporations, public bureaucracies, universities, and prisons are large and impersonal. In private corporations, managers and employees are competitively oriented, and are often viewed as more concerned about their own careers than about the problems of colleagues and customers. A deficit of humanistic concern is a problem for hospitals (Ravich, 1975; Ravich and Rehr, 1974) and universities as well as for major corporations. One essential goal of troubleshooting programs is therefore to increase the level of communication within organizations. Rowe and Baker (1984, p. 133) have described this service as follows:

> The commonest need of employees who request as-
> sistance is for information. Ways to defuse rumors, clarify

Figure 3. Complaint-Processing Diagram.

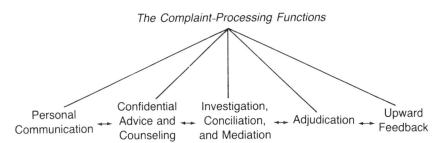

policy, and provide accurate information to employees who
have misunderstood a work situation are basic to a complaint system.

Supervisors out on the floor, responsible employee
networks, and sensitive human resources professionals may
perform this function. In many cases it is important to provide ways for employees to request information anonymously or confidentially.

The need for information is illustrated by our case study. In this
example, what would happen when other store clerks learn that the
woman was fired? To whom would they go to ask for clarification
if they were troubled about the ethics of the sales policy? And, most
important, to whom would the fired clerk turn for information
about response options—an attorney? The point is that problems
generate a need for additional information. Information is needed
by the sales clerk about company policy and about options, by her
sales colleagues, and (although he may not know it) by the
supervisor, who may have been wrong in his assumptions about the
level of support for unethical practices. This is why troubleshooters
emphasize communication—for the employee's sake, for the sake of
the organization's productivity, and for customer satisfaction.
Conflict and anxiety are productivity barriers that can sometimes be
removed by simple personal communication. For other problems,
anger and anxiety are the results of wrongs that require both redress
and advice. The refusal of a secretary or sales representative to cheat,
leading to their inappropriate termination, cannot be solved with
simple information.

Counseling An individual in great demand is a confidant
to talk to for both personal reasons and/or with respect to
organizational politics. Most people use work "buddies" or friends
in other units as counselors regarding their daily work problems,
their career aspirations, and the constant juggling required to
balance individual goals and objectives with those of the organization. Employees have personal problems that they do not want to
talk with colleagues about, but that are bothersome. They may need
nothing more than a good ear with commonsense advice, or they
may need a referral for more professional and prolonged assistance.

This kind of activity is a key one for troubleshooters. Rowe and Baker (1984, p. 133) have described it as follows: "Counseling can help address employees' lack of skill and lack of faith in responsible dispute resolution. One of the least dramatic but most effective things that employee counselors accomplish is to help both managers and employees see a problem in perspective, to frame and present it effectively, and to show them what options they have within the organization for resolving it. Most frequently the confidential counselor succeeds by helping a visitor resolve a problem on his or her own. Companies that take an innovative approach to complaint handling for nonunion employees are beginning to allow or encourage some confidential discussion of employee problems by supervisors as well as by personnel staff." The key point here is that counseling is of two different types. The troubleshooting is on a personal level. The troubleshooter acts as "friendly advisor" to clients requiring career guidance. The troubleshooter also acts in the role of professional referral agent— a diagnostician and resource person who matches client needs with internal and external resources such as EAP and private counseling.

For example, what does the fired store clerk do? Does she fight to change the system or just move on? There are pros and cons to both actions. Personal counseling and/or referral to a lawyer may be needed, although legal referrals are not made until all internal remedies are exhausted.

Customers use both formal and informal means to evaluate their options. Informally, they consult friends and co-workers at their place of business. What should they do with a defective product—a lemon automobile? What should they do about a physician error coupled with arrogance? Friends join them in their anger and say "sue." A customer relations troubleshooter can offer personal guidance on how to solve the problem in the most effective manner, often meaning without the expense and time delay of litigation.

However, in order to offer advice and counseling, the troubleshooter must have an understanding of the nature of the problem.

Investigation and Conflict Resolution   As noted in the opening chapters, *all* organizations have employee and customer complaints. Contrary to a belief that a lack of complaints is evidence of management skill, an organization without complaints is probably an organization that does not listen. The inclusion of problem investigation, conciliation, and mediation activity is a statement about the organization and what it feels is appropriate (its core values). Troubleshooter programs are one means by which employees and consumers can present their complaints to have them confronted by the organization. Their existence attests to management's recognition of the true reality of organizations: that all organizations have employees and customers who from time to time have complaints! The mature organization is one that is willing to admit to a reality with complaints, acting both to listen and to respond to voiced concerns. This reflects core values— concern for employee and customer problems—and organizational security in a psychological sense, since senior executives are mature enough to admit that they are not perfect (nor are others). A mature and sophisticated organizational culture constantly identifies and attempts to correct problems. Fact finding and conciliation are intimately linked with this activity, as we will see.

Rowe and Baker (1984, p. 133) have characterized the ideal process of investigation and mediation as follows: "A modern and creative approach to handling employee complaints stresses dispute resolution rather than adjudication. Many companies have procedures to investigate and mediate employee complaints in a far less polarized and formal manner than companies usually follow in unionized settings or when outside agencies are involved. The employee has to give permission for the investigation, which should be conducted on a low-key basis to protect everyone's privacy as well as the company's image." Many corporations, especially those with unions, already have formal grievance procedures, but these are often unsatisfactory. For example, they may be too formalized, adversarial in nature, time-consuming, bureaucratic, or quasi-legal; they may also involve labor contracts or promote win/lose outcomes. These characteristics contribute to the significant difficulty grievance systems experience in solving problems in a quick and effective fashion. There is a need for a less formal, less legalistic effort designed to solve problems through the use of negotiation and compromise. The informal troubleshooters and the more formal corporate or patient ombudsmen can cut through bureaucratic red tape, using much less formality in handling complaints.

When a representative of a formal grievance system enters a unit or department, you know automatically that it is likely to be a time-consuming, step-by-step process to resolution, with the outcome defined in terms of who is right and who is wrong. The emphasis of the troubleshooter is on problem solving and problem dissolving (Ackoff, 1981). The conditions for the problem are made to disappear. The investigation is not focused on the assignment of blame and the determination of right and wrong.

In the case of the sales clerk, is there not a possibility that the supervisor is completely mistaken in his view of the corporate sales policy? Is the problem simple—rehire the clerk, fire the supervisor—or is there a more complex solution that requires personal and organizational responses such as open discussion of policy and ethics and training to more positively treat the problem and prevent a recurrence?

Grievance systems make a formal determination of right and wrong. Troubleshooters do not. Troubleshooters do offer—however covert—a sense of whose position appears to be the more appropriate, though. This parallels but does not become adjudication.

Adjudication   Adjudicate means to judge and decide. If complaints are not handled by someone in the organization, they will be taken outside to a court where a judge will make a decision. Rowe and Baker (1984, p. 134) noted the following corporate concerns about adjudication in general: "Many companies have designed formal complaint and appeal channels for adjudication of complaints. Some are multistep systems designed to serve nonunion employees in unionized environments. As a result, they resemble traditional grievance systems in the scope and structure of their operations. A few such systems involve some form of binding arbitration that includes a neutral party from outside the company as a last step. This feature is said to be a critical aspect of the credibility and effectiveness of employee complaint procedures at companies such as American Electric Power, American Airlines, and TWA. . . ."

Many troubleshooters reject adjudication as an appropriate part of the job, since they do not feel that they should be responsible for deciding who is right and who is wrong. For example, many would refuse to serve as a "hearings judge" for the sales clerk/supervisor conflict. Instead, they regard themselves as facilitators of a problem resolution process whose success would depend in part on *not* assigning blame. In cases where troubleshooters do adjudicate disputes, the question of their fairness arises. Since troubleshooters are generally outside the line of supervision in organizations, there is the possibility that they could be biased against the individual's interests. However, there is a check to this bias. In practice, a constant tilting in favor of the organization would quickly dry up the stream of complaints. The employee grapevine is particularly efficient with regard to fairness. Employee and consumer perceptions that troubleshooters are biased would quickly kill the program.

Regardless of whether troubleshooters adjudicate disputes, a critical task is passing on information derived from the complaints of employees and consumers.

Feedback   One problem managers face is how to find out what's going on in their organizations. According to one survey (Kiechel, 1986), it is *the* most important problem for many executives. While managers have a general "interest" in getting the feel of the organization, the good ones also recognize that they really need to know what employees and consumers think in order to know how they are doing from the standpoint of management effectiveness, productivity, and the quality of working life. A complaint program that systematically processes employee and consumer complaints is one way to find out just what employees are thinking. This occurs through "upward feedback." Troubleshooters pass information to executives at the top levels of the organization, who become aware of what employees and consumers complain about and can use that data to help judge the successes and failures of the work system and products.

Troubleshooters are in fact part of a whole set of strategies for this purpose. Rowe and Baker (1984, p. 134) described the variety of programs used to obtain feedback as follows: "Companies use employee surveys, advisory councils, and formal and informal employee audits to stay alert to emerging problems. Many other structures can also contribute data. Quality circles can illuminate the employee relations issues that are often at the core of 'technical' problems. Health and safety committees (developed voluntarily or by federal law—that is, Washington) can identify supervisors or employees whose behavior poses a special risk. Mentoring arrangements provide a good ear and savvy advice on how the union employee should approach a problem encountered on the job; a summary of these problems is useful to management. Employee networks can help management understand the problems of special groups." The upward feedback of complaints about production processes, quality of working life issues, or productivity barriers means that the organization at least has an opportunity to address these problems, since of course the first step in solving any problem, whether personal or organizational, is knowing that the problem exists. Upward feedback provides the necessary data and sheds light on any patterns in existing problems. This helps executives assess whether there are differences between the organization's view of how it thinks it treats employees and customers and how it actually treats them (the "theories of action, theories in use" distinction of Argyris and Schon, 1975). Upward feedback is one way to facilitate the organizational learning process.

In summary, complaint processing—the troubleshooter's primary activity—involves personal communication; confidential advice and counseling; investigation, conciliation, and mediation; adjudication; and upward feedback. As we have observed, all of these functions are interrelated.

Education and Training

The second major component of the troubleshooter's job is education and training. Education is defined as instruction given to individuals or groups to prepare and/or update them for work—the work of production or the "work" of consuming goods and services. Troubleshooters provide preparatory and/or continuing education to employees or consumers in both formal and informal ways. They help to educate employees early in their career, and they can also

provide seasoned employees with additional training. More
specifically, troubleshooters educate four groups: (1) employees
who complain, (2) the subjects of those complaints, (3) upper
management, and (4) colleagues in the human problem response
group—employee assistance staff, customer relations representatives, and others.

Continuing Education Troubleshooters provide continuing education because managers, employees, and customers already
have knowledge and experience about the company. This represents
a base on which the educational efforts of troubleshooters can build.
Shortell's (1978) comments suggest the need to develop an ability to
continually acquire new skills and knowledge and confront value
positions.

Troubleshooters provide continuing education and training
on an almost unlimited number of topics. The list is defined by the
subjects of the complaints. The job and work experience of the sales
clerk are just one of the topics. The involvement of troubleshooters
in the sales clerk's problem produces continuing education for both
the clerk and the supervisor, for example regarding policy acceptance and review of termination. It may also educate a few upper
managers about the "trickle down" of corporate goals and values
(hopefully a negative aspect uncovered). Each educational initiative
is most significant for the individual and simultaneously has
benefits for the organization as a whole. The clerk will be educated
about her conflict. The supervisor may get "educated" about his
interpretation of corporate sales policy. And some senior managers
may get an education about what is happening in the trenches.

Some of this education can be converted to training that
works to prevent future occurrence of these problems. Along with
continuing education, then, some troubleshooters provide preparatory education.

Preparatory Education Troubleshooters also provide preparatory education, both in the intellectual sense and with respect
to individual skills. For example, they may become involved in
providing basic job readiness training for new managers. At this
stage of their careers, these managers need to learn about work

attitudes, conflict resolution, and productivity requirements. They must also acquire basic skills in customer and employee relations. Troubleshooters have considerable experience and skill in these areas, and so are in an excellent position to provide preparatory training.

Educating senior management is often not labeled education but consultation, the final core activity of troubleshooters.

Consultation

Troubleshooters are consultants to senior management and to the participants in the conflicts they are called on to help resolve. In my view, troubleshooters are internal consultants. The designation *internal consultant* includes a wide range of consulting activities and consultant definitions. The following was offered by Meyers, Alpert, and Fleisher (1983): "There seems to be agreement that consultation is a joint effort at problem solving and that consultation involves indirect assistance of a third party. While there is agreement around these general issues, the models differ with respect to such issues as the role of the consultant, the problems to be addressed in consultation, and the means to go about helping. The theoretical framework and assumptions underlying each particular type of consultation naturally lead to these differences." There is no convenient classification system for the varieties of consultation models in troubleshooting, but all approaches and models involve some form of joint problem solving. The approaches taken by consultants—and, by implication, troubleshooters—differ: "While other models are content-oriented, organization development is form-oriented. Thus, its goal is not content specific; rather, it is . . . to help train members of organizations to be able to make the changes they democratically see fit to make on a system, not individual, level. Through fostering increased understanding of interpersonal communication, the uncovering of conflicts and interdependence, the increase in the desire and the ability to establish collective goals and make decisions, the OD consultant facilitates the development of a self-renewing system" (Meyers, Alpert, and Fleisher, 1983, p. 7).

In practical terms, a number of consultant types were defined by the Organization Development Institute for the benefit of its members' clients, distinctions that also describe the troubleshooters' consulting options. Troubleshooters can act as *purchase of service consultants,* as *expert advice consultants,* and/or as *process consultants.* The first of these are the consultants who provide a set of "packages" that can be applied in general fashion to a wide group of organizational problems. Examples of problems or needs that can often use set programs are time management or team building. Or a troubleshooter involved with a whole series of cases relating to the ethics of sales policy (such as the clerk's dilemma) may decide to offer a half-day workshop to supervisors and managers. This might be designed and developed as a one-time effort or repeated throughout the organization. The troubleshooter may be a consultant to the designers of the workshop and/or a member of the team using the case experience for training. While there are troubleshooters that could easily offer this service— particularly after years on the job—few spend much time providing standard packages of education and training. Since troubleshooters nearly always confront unique problems in new situations, prepackaged solution programs would rarely if ever work.

Troubleshooters also offer expert advice based on their intimate knowledge of the organization and their knowledge of problem solving and conflict resolution. The expert consultant is called in to diagnose a problem and to provide knowledgeable advice on how to respond. Data gathering and a report are key. The report makes direct suggestions and recommendations for action based on the expert's specialist knowledge of the problem and subject area. Troubleshooters "visit" many parts of the organization during their complaint handling. They observe and interview and report not only on the specific case but on the issues of concern to the organization, the patterns of problems that seem to be emerging. They are experts on problem pattern analysis and data feedback and on problem resolution.

Delivering expert assessments and providing packaged training or services are both very different from process consulting, which I feel is the key consulting role for troubleshooters. This is the third type of troubleshooter consultant work and the Organization Development Institute's preferred consulting approach: "The third consultant type, the *Process Consultant,* is again a professional group or individual who focuses attention on how work is accomplished. This is the usual model espoused by the Organization Development professional. In this consultant model, an organization diagnosis is made, the results of the diagnosis are shared with staff and management, and the needs of the organization are identified, clarified, and put in perspective. Next, the consultant determines, in collaboration with the organization, which problems are most immediate and what has to be learned or done in order to correct these. The consultant, again in concert with staff, will create an intensive learning program especially designed to meet the individual organization's needs. After the program is planned, conducted and evaluated, new learning programs are created and the cycle begins anew" (Organization Development Institute, 1981). The troubleshooter as process consultant is the organizational development consultant referred to by Meyers, Alpert, and Fleisher (1983), defined in detail by Schein (1969), and illustrated by Hirschhorn and Krantz (1982).

While some troubleshooters may offer prepackaged programs, most act as process consultants when providing consulting service in their troubleshooter role. Some troubleshooters have expert knowledge, for example on conflict resolution and sexual harassment, but they are not used as often in their organizations for their technical expertise as for their abilities in helping others solve problems. The troubleshooter assists in creating a process that will (1) resolve individual client complaints and problems (employee and/or customer), and (2) initiate diagnostic assessment that will help to create learning and response actions for the organization as a whole. Troubleshooters work *with* employees and managers to continue the organization's development. They are not assigned responsibility for action; that remains with line and staff personnel.

For the sales clerk problem, the question is whether the organization will investigate further to determine how widespread the problem is. How will the need for this process be promoted and sold? Troubleshooters act as consultants to management, offering ideas and facilitating the process of problem confrontation and resolution.

Neutrality

When troubleshooters work at complaint processing, education, and consultation, are they neutral or are they agents of the corporation or agents (advocates) of the client? This is a significant question. Rowe (1987, p. 128) reviews this issue as follows:

> An ombudsman clearly is *not* an ordinary kind of advocate: this practitioner specifically is not a conventional "employee advocate." But the definitions of "neutrality" and "impartiality" adopted by practitioners vary from company to company.
>
> About half the companies with ombuds offices have designated their practitioners as neutrals. Nearly all expect the practitioner to be at least impartial in all interpersonal interactions, including those with senior managers. (All expect the practitioner to uphold relevant laws, statutes and company policies; one is, in other words, not "neutral" with regard to the law or company policy.)
>
> Practitioners tend to talk about these matters in company-specific terms, such as:
>
> "I am an advocate for fair *process*, not for any specific person or position."
>
> "I am impartial and neutral up to the point that I find a law or company policy being flouted."
>
> "My company believes the long-range interests of the company lie with anyone who has been unfairly treated. If two people have each treated the other unfairly, the company may have an interest on both sides."
>
> Most practitioners simply say, "I have to find solutions that meet many sets of rights and interests," or "The ombudsman will take into account the rights of all employees and managers and the obligations of the company . . . and also the rights of the company and the obligations of employees and managers." In technical terminology, the ombudsman is committed to integrative solutions, and avoids distributive solutions both by the design of the office (an informal nonadjudicatory structure) and by personal commitment.

Acting neutral in order that clients perceive the troubleshooter to be fair and impartial is critical to the job. Whether a troubleshooter (or formal ombudsman) is officially designated as a "neutral" is almost irrelevant. Perceived and real neutrality is essential to the successful carrying out of the job.

Troubleshooter Job Characteristics

A few more brief comments on the characteristics of the trouble-shooter's job are warranted. A desirable job design has seven characteristics (Umstot, Mitchell, and Bell, 1978; Kast and Rosenzweig, 1985) that can be cited for review purposes:

1. There is very high *skill variety*, with troubleshooters using a wide range of skills and talents in almost every case.
2. Troubleshooters have responsibility for the case from start to finish. They assume responsibility for problem resolution (*task identity*).
3. The job itself has great meaning for both the individual with the problem and the organization (*task significance*). Both suffer from the conflict.
4. Troubleshooters have considerable *autonomy*, since they need freedom and discretion in order to get the job done.
5. *Feedback* from clients and superiors is both clear and direct. Conflicts are resolved or they escalate.
6. Troubleshooters' goals are clear (*goal clarity*). They must resolve conflicts for personal and organizational benefits.
7. But *goal difficulty* is high, meaning that there is constant challenge in the job.

These seven characteristics describe why the troubleshooter's job is both highly stimulating and enticing. It is meaningful, important, and highly challenging, the kind of job in which one gets deeply involved.

The Flow of Work Activity

What is the flow of these troubleshooter actions? An executive might ask whether troubleshooters provide each of these services to all employees and customers in some sort of flow sequence. In fact,

Figure 4. Two-Client Activity Track.

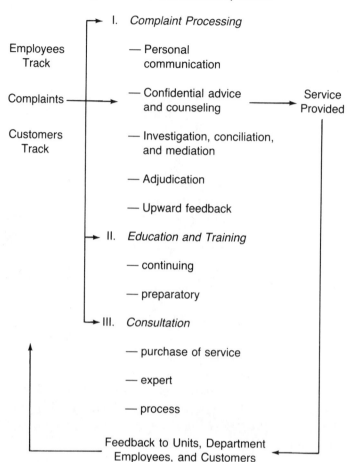

they do not. The work in each case is most often unique, although there are repetitions of problem-solving paths.

For organizations that are collecting complaints from both employees and customers, the troubleshooter activities can be thought of as a two-track process, as shown in Figure 4. On the one hand, complaints from employees and/or customers are taken in. The transformation process (in systems terms) involves the primary work activities of complaint processing (personal communication; confidential advice and counseling; investigation, conciliation, and mediation; adjudication; and upward feedback), education and training (continuing, preparatory), and consultation (service, expert, process). The outputs include information that is passed on to executives regarding the nature of structure and process difficulties in the organization.

Summary

This chapter defined the troubleshooter's job as consisting of three core activities: complaint processing, education and training, and consultation. Complaint processing involves personal communication; confidential advice and counseling; investigation, conciliation, and mediation; adjudication; and upward feedback. Troubleshooter educational activity involves providing both continuing and preparatory education to employees and customers. Troubleshooters inform employees about the nature of conditions, policies, and rules in the organization and about the effects of their own behavior. Upward feedback is used for educating top management about the status of the organization's employees and customers (that is, whether they are satisfied or not) and about the organization's production performance. Finally, consultation is provided, with process work being the dominant consulting role.

4

Designing and Implementing a Troubleshooter Program

How do we begin? We use another example to illustrate.

Sexual Harassment

Susan Davidson was a professional secretary with ambition and determination. She had top flight skills and was finishing a bachelor's degree in business at night. She wanted a promotion to an administrative position. When her boss's administrative officer announced she was leaving in two months, Susan informed Mr. Thompson she was interested. He said she was qualified and a hard worker and suggested a meeting to review the job and her other qualifications. He suggested dinner, which she politely declined, preferring instead to talk in the office. One week later he suggested dinner again, getting the same response from her. When all the candidates were selected for interviews, she was not in the group. When she inquired why, Mr. Thompson said she "did not measure up." She sued.

How does an employee solve this kind of problem? Davidson solved it by suing the company—and winning. When she started, she had no "hate" for the company, only anger about the way she was treated. However, when her company refused to address her problem, her anger about unfair treatment led her to the courts. This is one way the need for a troubleshooter program is identified.

This chapter deals with the creation of troubleshooting programs. Since formal types are most complex, it focuses on formal programs; a few brief remarks are also devoted to informal programs. We turn first to the formal start-up process, which is initially discussed as if we were walking through a program planning team's analysis.

A Formal Troubleshooter Program's Beginning

How troubleshooting programs get started is an interesting story with many variations. One corporation ignored complaints from employees and customers that resulted in lawsuits ultimately costing several million dollars. In any severe case—from denial of promotion to sabotage and harassment—the costs eventually include aggravation for executives, the loss of one or two persons fired, heavy emotional stress, and unproductive work time with resulting dollar losses from senior executives' involvement in the case.

Organizations also have a long-term fear that bigger complaints will eventually surface. For example, company managers with several divisions developing chemicals used in fertilizers worried that some employees in the plant would feel that their concerns about job safety were not being heard. Employees might go to the courts with the problem, generating a lawsuit like the ones involving asbestos. The managers thought that if they could respond to and correct individual safety complaints, they could avoid major conflicts by resolving individual disputes at an early stage.

Program start-up is also stimulated when executives are astonished to find that they could lose so much money on "small matters" such as sexual harassment. Their surprise leads to an attitude of, "What if we had a real problem here?" This is a fairly common position, not particular to any executive group. As the financial and personal costs of settlements rise, this position is changing and so are large corporations' responses to complaints.

A question leading to program discussions is therefore how to reduce future litigation, both from employees and from dissatisfied or wronged customers. A wrongful termination case is an example. Management debate about options in one case usually leads to the need to explore alternative ways of resolving disputes within the corporation and between the corporation and outside parties. This prompts discussion of dispute resolution techniques and of the ongoing national search for alternatives to litigation.

Although it is an interesting subject for executives, few have information on the nature and development of new approaches to conflict resolution. At best, perhaps one staff member will have heard about the growing interest in troubleshooting programs in private corporations. Those with some experience in public affairs may know of the ombudsman role in government agencies. There is often no immediate direction to proceed, however. The executive taking a formal approach to development might appoint a program planning team to proceed through a series of development steps. While each process is unique, five typical steps are as follows:

Step 1: Conduct environmental analysis—the external view.

Step 2: Assess fit with corporate culture—the organization's internal status.

Step 3: Design the troubleshooter program.

Step 4: Start up and operate.

Step 5: Periodically evaluate progress.

These steps are similar to the program planning used for any new product or service (for example, see Scheirer, 1981; Posavac and Carey, 1985). To assist readers in understanding the troubleshooter program planning process and to provide some guidelines for program development, each step is reviewed in some detail.

Step 1: Conduct Environmental Analysis—The External View

A planning group for a troubleshooter program may first conduct a "scan of the organizational environment" as the initial formal program planning activity. Two or three members will assess whether the current external environment will support an alternative dispute resolution system. Through a series of meetings, the planning group will scan the environmental areas for support or rejection of the troubleshooter concept. These areas would include such topics as law, culture, technology, education, and politics.

Troubleshooter program planners must determine whether general external environmental trends support a complaint mechanism as a useful addition to the organization. It is an attractive activity *if* it can help to avoid outcomes such as the cost of the sexual harassment settlement. But beyond cost savings, what does a troubleshooter program accomplish, either positively or negatively, that would generate support or resistance from the environment? Members of the planning team might divide their scanning into the areas of the organizational environment that we have surveyed earlier (law, economics, technology, politics, and so on).

After a series of meetings and extensive research, a memorandum will emerge that identifies the degree of fit between the proposed troubleshooter program and current trends in the business and public arenas. The following review is illustrative of this scanning activity and its output.

EXHIBIT 1

MEMORANDUM
To: Senior Executive Group
From: Troubleshooter Program Planning Group
Re: Environmental Review

Background. We were asked to examine the troubleshooter concept because the company is faced with increasing litigation, and it has dual interests in improving the quality of working life and removing barriers to productivity. This part of our report addresses external issues.

Analysis. The first area we reviewed was the *law.* There are some current trends and considerations of great interest to the corporation. Recent settlements of wrongful termination and sexual harassment cases (among many other types) are increasingly recognized for their legal and economic impact. But further probing uncovered other legal issues for the organization.

Many private corporations and public agencies have always used outside counsel. However, the growth in outside counsel's expenses has been phenomenal, especially over the past ten years. Both private and public organizations are seeking ways to diminish the use of outside counsel. Recently, they have begun to build their own complement of internal corporate legal staff. In some organizations, management has announced the need for a program for reducing legal costs. Many organizations have grasped the fact that there must be alternatives to court settlements of issues and problems related to corporate activities. It is clear that legal pressures in the organizational environment are pushing for alternative ways to settle disputes. This one area of the organizational environment shows support for troubleshooter development.

Closely allied to this is *economics,* the second subject of our scanning. In many organizations, there already is recognition of the high cost of ignored complaints. There is no "environmental data" indicating that future complaints will be lower in numbers or that the financial impact will be lessened. If anything, prevailing experience suggests that as higher settlements in suits of all types begin to emerge, they become "data" for analysis by certain interested parties (potential plaintiffs and their attorneys). This is illustrated by the medical malpractice cases. Both attorneys and future complainants tend to watch the size of the settlements and, in some cases, the ease with which they are arrived at, using these observations to determine their future interest in pressing a case.

In short, it appears that all organizations' costs of handling complaints—either by ignoring them or by allowing them to go to court—will eventually become unacceptably high.

A part of this concern about complaints stems from the general recognition that *culturally* (the third environmental area) more employees and customers are becoming assertive about their individual rights. The rise in corporate legal expenses and in part the increase in legal involvement in customer and employee concerns is a cultural phenomenon. More consumers are concerned about their rights and about producer obligations. This was initiated with the widely known activities of Ralph Nader. It has continued more recently in the direction of employees' rights (Ewing, 1977; Westin and Salisbury, 1980; Ewing, 1983). This change in employee/consumer assertiveness will be an increasing problem as more members of the culture *believe* that they have employee/consumer rights that they can assert. In short, the changing American culture will be a contributor to an increase in complaints in the future.

This cultural trend toward more complaints is linked to the increasing *educational* level of the population (a fourth environmental area). Although there is relatively little data, the speculation is that those people most likely to complain are those most educated about their rights and the demands that they can make on public and private organizations. The rising educational level of the population is thus seen as a potential contributor to an increase in complaints. This educational level creates a need for a formal mechanism to allow educated persons to voice their concerns and to have a fair hearing. Additionally, educated persons are less likely to be fooled by or satisfied with the public relations–oriented activities of corporations and their image-making representatives. In short, an educated population is more likely to see through a corporation's superficial attempts to smooth over or finesse a problem, resulting in further complaints or a quick trip to the courts.

The hi-tech future is a part of the fifth environmental area. The educational level of the population is related to the phenomenal growth in *technologies* in almost all organizations. This phenomenal growth is hardly surprising, nor is it thought to be a situation that will either disappear or level off. Along with technological growth comes an increase in the sophistication of the work force and the complexity of the work systems. Both sophistication and complexity result in more potential areas and points for conflict between the organization and employees and consumers. It is assumed that the rise in technology and the change generated by the inclusion of new technology in existing work systems will create much employee anxiety and, inevitably, complaints about the way the organization responds to these problems. Additionally, increases in new technology yield problems in new-product performance and in product understanding and use by consumers. Technology is thus considered a primary contributor to the expected future growth in complaints.

Politics is the next environmental topic. In past years, there has been a belief that government in one form or another would step in to help resolve individual versus organization conflicts, or at least would offer a mechanism for doing so. However, politics in the 1980s is following a trend away from government intervention. While this does not yet have long-standing continuity, this trend can become semipermanent. It appears in the late 1980s to have crossed party lines a bit, leading to a sense that government will be reducing or, at the most, maintaining the status quo with regard to conflict intervention. This translates into a need for organizations to create their own mechanisms for responding to complaints. Waiting for government to offer the *President's Council on Employee Conflict Resolution* and/or a design for the *Federal Complaint Resolution System* would seem to be a risky venture. Since these are unlikely and not even on the horizon, organizations would lose much time waiting for a model system to emerge, particularly given time requirements for research and development. In short, the politics of help from the public sector seems to be both distant and uncertain. Self-help conflict resolution appears to be necessary.

Two final environmental trends are significant but less primary contributors to the pressure for troubleshooter programs. One environmental pressure is *sociological*. Human resource staff are especially aware of the changing patterns of relationships among employees and the emerging stresses of all sorts, such as two-career families, for example. This has generated difficulties in transfer and hiring/recruitment. It is expected that these changes in the work force will continue to place upward pressure on conflict levels. For example, the pure logistical difficulties of transferring two career-oriented employees means that corporations will experience more complaints about movement of employees around national and worldwide sites.

Related sociological changes include a "back-to-roots" and "family life" orientation that makes corporate employees less open to transfer. At any point of difference between "usual organizational behavior" (for example, openness to transfer) and an employee's new sociological changes/directions, there is increased conflict potential.

The final concern for troubleshooter program planning is the issue of *demography*. The aging of the population means that at some point the corporation will again have to address issues such as mandatory retirement. While organizations are moving to resolve this with competency-based tests and other mechanisms, the problem of how to manage increasing numbers of aging employees is pressing. Consider the educational level of the population now and the increased sophistication in the next twenty to thirty years when the baby boom generation ages. Is it not more likely that this group will be inclined to act in its own interests, presenting complaints to the corporation's management about the way they are treated? Phenomenal growth in the aging group is expected. The gradual emergence of the aging population's power means that this is an environmental pressure that should not be understated. Planning to manage the complaints they generate is critical.

While this list is not an exhaustive scan of our corporate environment, it does show significant pressures for development of a mechanism for resolving complaints. The planning group has sufficient evidence to suggest that systems designs should be explored. In fact, several pressures (for example, legal and economic) are independently significant enough to generate support for a troubleshooter program, irrespective of the contributions of the other pressure points.

After this environmental scan, the program planning group needs to determine how well a troubleshooter program concept fits their organizational culture. This leads the group to analyze the organizational culture, with attention directed toward the degree of fit between culture, the company's current status, and the troubleshooter program concept.

Step 2: Assess Fit with Corporate Culture—The Organization's Internal Status

A *culture review* or *culture audit* is an analysis of the match between the organization's characteristics and the troubleshooter concept. The planning group concentrates on defining and describing the five items listed below:

- participants and their characteristics
- occupations of the work group
- power and specific interest groups
- general organizational characteristics
- corporate trends and current financial status

The purpose of this internal analysis is to determine whether the organization would accept a troubleshooter program and whether the timing is right. With the help of brainstorming sessions, the above topics are expanded, using this list as the starting elements for consideration. All of these are reviewed, with the highlights of the findings presented in a summary memorandum.

Participants and Characteristics   The planning group first considers who in the corporate culture would have a stake in a new problem resolution system (a stakeholder analysis; Mitroff, 1983). The analysis begins at the top, focusing on the chief executive officer and senior vice presidents (or their equivalent in public sector management: secretaries of cabinet-level departments and their deputies). These individuals need to believe in and support the troubleshooter concept right from the start in order for it to become viable. The chief executive officer must believe in employee/ consumer communication and be willing to back it with resources. The planning group must determine whether the CEO has a management group that will tolerate and, more important, encourage open communication. Communication between management and employees up and down the organization needs to be supported, since without this communication base, the troubleshooter concept has no chance.

In order for the planning group to feel that top management is open to the concept, they must find a troubleshooter program to be a logical extension of management's philosophy and activity within the organization. How, for example, does management usually address issues like policy conflict, interpersonal conflict, and alcoholism? Are the problems openly confronted and addressed? Or are they submerged and ignored? If a key member of the senior executive team is violently opposed to open confrontation of complaints, start-up will be difficult.

The planning group must also consider the views of middle management and employees. Are they accustomed to a culture that encourages open dialogue and communication? When the program concept is announced to the employees and to consumers, will they see this as an attempt to *continue* to solicit employee suggestions and complaints, or will it be new?

In summary, will a troubleshooter program be consistent with most of the personal philosophies of management and employees that define the organizational culture as a whole? If not, the troubleshooter program will be an intended (or unintended) part of cultural change—from closed to open communication—with all of the attendant problems that major change entails.

For example, the secretary in our opening case can take her complaint to a troubleshooter (new to the company) as the "first case" to be openly addressed *ever*. The level of shock will be much higher than in a company where problems and issues were confronted and resolved by a peer review program (Olson, 1984) or other complaint system (Rowe and Baker, 1984).

Occupations   A second planning area involves employee occupations. Are there occupations that do not fit with the troubleshooting concept? We know that troubleshooters are at work in organizations where there is a mix of highly sophisticated engineers and research and development personnel (Bell Labs), in those with manufacturing personnel (McDonnell Douglas), in those where production-oriented clerks (Blue Shield) or assembly line workers (General Motors) are dominant, and in a wide range of public agencies (welfare departments, hospitals). The program is most consistent with a work force that has experienced openness, including opportunities to speak out and be heard.

Some organizations would not allow discussion of a sexual harassment case. Others would discuss it as an individual *personal* problem of one employee. Troubleshooters need at least enough freedom from the culture to support confronting the problem as a single case, and as a possible organization-wide issue.

Power and Interest Groups   The planning group must address the question of power. This design issue involves the need to have the troubleshooter report to someone high in the organization, someone with enough authority and power to permit the troubleshooter to do his or her work. In many organizations, the chief executive officer is the logical choice. Unfortunately, many top executives have a passion for attending meetings in other cities, for making themselves highly visible to their divisions throughout the country and to community and professional groups. Given this situation, practicality often means that the CEO is not the choice for troubleshooter supervisor. Instead, a frequent choice is the senior vice president for human resources, since troubleshooting in the context presented in this book is predominantly people-oriented.

This is sometimes not a good choice, since power in private corporations does not always rest with human resources/personnel people. However, when a chief executive officer with tenure and recognized performance personally supports the senior vice president for human resources, the setup will work. When human resources has the ear of the CEO and this fact is well known, he or she is a good choice for a power base for the troubleshooter. Few other formal positions lower in the organization are thought to be viable as troubleshooter reporting links.

Regardless of the position, power and reporting relationship are interlocked, and depend on a good relationship between the troubleshooter and the executive to whom he or she reports. With a good relationship, a troubleshooter can present and discuss sensitive cases such as suicide, sabotage, and sexual harassment. Without that relationship, those cases will not be addressed or even brought to light.

General Organizational Characteristics; Finances   The fourth area for consideration is the fit between the troubleshooter concept and certain organizational characteristics; the fifth area involves finances. Here the planning group offers its review in a memorandum.

EXHIBIT 2

MEMORANDUM
To: Senior Executive Group
From: Troubleshooter Program Planning Group
Re: Organization's Status

　　Purpose. We reviewed the organization's current status to assess the degree of fit between where the company is now and the troubleshooter concept. This memo covers three areas—history, character, and financial status and trend.

History. The organization has been in business since 1910. It has experienced no labor/management difficulties but has operated for its full history without a union. There are some 35,000 employees in this particular branch of the organization. The corporation holds a 32 percent market share in a market that is fairly competitive—a dominant share. The company was founded by a family who turned over management of the business to professional managers some twenty years ago but still maintains large stock holdings. They tend not to interfere in the business. It is not expected that the board would have any difficulties with the addition of a troubleshooter.

Character. The corporation tends to be activist-oriented in terms of public positions in support of environmental protection, community development, outdoor recreation activities, and general community services. The corporation has a long-established and excellent community reputation, both within its geographical locale and in the national business community. The program planning group feels that corporate members and family stockholders would not be concerned about the potential for "bad image" publicity if someone found out they had a "complaint taker." If the media discovered that the corporation allowed employees to file complaints, it would be an indicator that the corporation had the courage to confront the issues, typical of its earned reputation.

In short, this organization's history and character were viable and healthy in early periods and they are today. A financial review of the corporation reinforces this status.

Financial Status and Trend. The corporation seems to be in a significant growth trend. Its financial status was termed "very healthy." There is no question that the corporation could financially afford the addition of a non-revenue-producing position. The planning team believes that this kind of issue would not even arise for discussion. Profits for the past year were the second best in the organization's history. Financially, the timing is right for making an addition to the problem-solving mechanisms of the corporation. It would be regarded as moving forward in a positive, future-oriented sense and can be billed as a mechanism that would remove potential negative impacts on the future bottom line.

In summary, the planning group's brief review of these internal characteristics of the organization (participants, occupations, power, internal characteristics, and finances) indicated that there were no obstacles to the design and development of this troubleshooter program. In fact, the timing appeared to be quite appropriate for the addition of the program to the organization.

The planning group next outlined the goals, technical system, and management design for the troubleshooter program. This was a participative process that involved senior management, middle managers, and employees.

Step 3: Design the Troubleshooter Program

Planning must encompass the actual design of the troubleshooter program, although not yet the operational issues, the day-to-day activities of the troubleshooters. The purpose of this planning is to develop an overview of the goals, technical work, structural arrangements, and management of the program. This analysis is divided into five areas of planning work, according to one model of organization and management (Kast and Rosenzweig, 1985). The planning group must define the program's (1) goals, values, and culture; (2) technical activities; (3) structure; (4) psychosocial aspects; and (5) management. This is an organizational systems analysis of the troubleshooter program (Ziegenfuss, 1985c, 1985a). The following overview details typical findings of a troubleshooter planning group with respect to design issues.

Goals, Values, and Culture   A first planning consideration involves defining the philosophy and nature of the program, including the culture it will promote. What are the purposes of the program? How would the mission and purposes of a new trouble-shooter program fit with the culture of the organization?

As a start, the planning group must establish that the mission of the program is a developmental one. There should be complete agreement that the values and philosophy of the program are "helping," not "policing" in orientation. The problem resolution program should be *designed* for the purpose of helping the organization. It helps by assisting employees and management to resolve barriers to productivity and it helps by increasing the quality of working life and the quality of consuming life. Some investigation-type complaint programs are established with policing functions; their primary purpose is accountability, which may conflict with the helping mission of the troubleshooter.

We have seen that the objectives of troubleshooting programs are to increase employee productivity, communication, and participation, and to improve the quality of working life. These goals in turn imply certain values: (1) the sharing of problem responsibility and open communication, (2) employee and consumer participation, (3) a commitment to a high quality of employee work life, and (4) open confrontation of both individual and organizational problems. These values are represented by the "rituals" of complaint confrontation and resolution that become embedded in the corporate culture (Schein, 1985).

Rites and rituals are the "culture transmission method" that communicate the goals and values of the troubleshooter program to managers and employees, a means for establishing the program's presence on a regular basis. For example, once a month the troubleshooter is invited to the senior executive meeting (a usual ritual) to present a critique of the kinds of complaints (such as policy problems, personnel complaints, and harassment) and the types of resolutions used (for example, negotiated compromise, reprimand for manager, department-wide training). A second example of embedding the troubleshooter's work in existing rituals is to make the complaint summaries a part of the executives' quarterly and six-month reports that are reviewed in depth by the executive team. Through formal presentations and informal discussions, this establishes the troubleshooter's presence in the organization, ensuring his or her place in the cultural network of senior executives.

The presence of the troubleshooter in the cultural network involves several concerns. How does he or she fit into the structure (for example, at what level), and how is acceptance established? This individual must have access to senior management meetings on a regular basis, needing only to notify senior management that he or she would be attending. If real top-executive support exists, this should be affirmed most of the time. Troubleshooters invest time in senior management meetings, both as a way of marketing the adviser service and as a way of getting to know key executives.

There are two useful networks to which the troubleshooter must be connected. The first is the senior management group just discussed. The second network is the human resources group. This group includes human resources personnel such as the employee assistance program people, personnel counselors, and the EEO representative. Involvement in this network is not so important for power and status in the organization. Instead, this is the group of working relationships that will generate referrals and linkages for the troubleshooter program, for example referral of a complaining employee with an addiction problem to the employee assistance representative or referral of a policy problem from EAP to the troubleshooter. Without close and ongoing linkage to the executive network, there will be no power and authority. Without linkage to the human resource network, there will be no referral sources or resources for support.

We have reviewed goals, values, and troubleshooter linkage to the cultural network that already exists. There is an alternative to harmony with the existing culture. The issue of whether or not the troubleshooter program would initiate cultural change within the organization must be addressed.

One basic question with regard to cultural maintenance or change is whether the presence of the troubleshooter indicates a move toward much higher levels of employee/management or consumer/corporation communication. Some organizations have very open communication and operations as a starting point. In these there is little fear that a troubleshooter would be a contradiction to the corporate culture. In public and private organizations with open communication, the presence of the troubleshooter simply formalizes the openness that already exists, creating a good match between the existing organizational culture and the new position. For an organization interested in moving toward a more participative, open culture, the troubleshooter becomes a part of the change process. Instead of repressing complaints, they are now brought out and addressed directly, often meaning that initial discomfort with the troubleshooter will be high. In a "closed

culture," the sexual harassment case is quietly resolved by suggesting that the secretary leave or transfer to another division. With a
push for cultural openness, this case is still confidentially solved,
but the issue is raised on a corporate level (without disclosure of the
parties involved). Problems and issues can acquire a high profile as
needed. In organizations with closed cultures, on the other hand,
fierce resistance to a new program of this type would be expected.
Where cultural change is the agenda, a plan will be needed if the
troubleshooter program is part of a planned change effort.

　　This completes the review of troubleshooter program goals,
values, and culture issues. The troubleshooter represents goals and
values that may or may not be a part of the existing corporate
culture. If not, cultural change is an intended or unintended
outcome. Planning must assess this starting point before moving to
the technical design questions, the next planning topic.

　　Technical Troubleshooter Activities　Planning must address a series of design questions. Troubleshooter program design
involves eight topics:

- determining the target group of clients
- specifying the primary duties of the troubleshooter
- defining allowable complaint topics
- selecting problem resolution techniques
- setting the degree of formality of the effort
- establishing confidentiality guidelines
- providing feedback on individual and complaint groups
- defining data use

All program elements are more fully detailed later, but it is
important to define some broad guidelines for these technical issues
from the start. Each is briefly described in the memo that follows,
a sample of how one corporation might present the operational
design for a troubleshooter program for employees. The topics are
identical for a customer-oriented program; they only need to be
altered to fit the consumer focus.

EXHIBIT 3

MEMORANDUM
To: Senior Executive Group
From: Troubleshooter Program Planning Group
Re: Troubleshooter Program Technical Design

This memorandum addresses eight technical design elements of our proposed troubleshooter program.

1. *Target Group of Employees.* The troubleshooter is to be used by all nonunion employees at all levels except top management. Union employees in the various divisions have their own formal grievance program. Top management executives are excluded. They would not be able to get much satisfaction by complaining to a troubleshooter who reports to a colleague. Additionally, the conflict of interest inherent in the troubleshooter working for one colleague while taking complaints from another would not be functional.

2. *Primary Duties.* The planning group considered *Harvard Business Review* articles by Silver (1967) and Rowe and Baker (1984) that outlined duties of the corporate ombudsman. These are seen as good starting descriptions of the complaint program, which could evolve and be adapted as necessary over time. The functions included the following:

A. Complaint processing
    1. personal communication
    2. confidential advice and counseling
    3. investigation, conciliation, and mediation
    4. adjudication
    5. upward feedback
B. education and training
C. consultation

These are considered to be the primary activities of the new troubleshooter.

3. *Complaint Topics.* The types of complaints to be taken comprise the third technical design topic. It was decided that the scope of complaint topics would *not* be narrow. There should be wide latitude in choice in the interest of stimulating complaints and in avoiding the problem of a single type of complaint being the "identifier" for the system. The design team is interested in promoting the use

of the system; attempting to define excluded topics would decrease utilization.

The group brainstormed a sample list of expected employee complaint subjects as follows:

- promotion
- discrimination
- sexual harassment
- policies
- benefits
- personality conflicts
- unfair treatment generally
- dismissal practices
- physical environment

It was expected that this list would expand, with the topic boundaries being nearly unlimited. However, it was recognized that if the company developed related programs like employee assistance and equal opportunity, some of the complaints taken by the troubleshooter would be referred to one of these offices for a response. This would limit the troubleshooter's time in these areas to complaint identification and referral.

4. *Techniques.* The planning group addressed the question of whether this program would be primarily an interpersonal type of response in terms of complaint investigation and follow-up. The option at the other end of the method continuum was to create a paper- and pencil-based system. MIT has an ombudsman who uses a person-to-person approach (Rowe, 1987), while some companies, like American Express, have letter-based systems (American Express Company, 1982). Others such as Control Data have a telephone-based system.

The design group recognized that it was possible to establish a complaint program using either type of technique, that is, heavy personal interaction on an in-person basis, or paper and pencil letter writing and response (or telephone contact). However, the design group felt that the primary technique should involve individual interpersonal exchange. This was recognized as a much more expensive design but one that would ultimately establish more intensive communication within the organization.

5. *Degree of Formality.* The design group felt that the troubleshooter program should maintain a high level

of informality. While complaint processes should be documented, it was important to keep it relatively informal in order to stay away from the "legalistic" complaint resolution system designs. It was generally assumed that all troubleshooter programs face internal *ongoing pressures* toward increasing documentation and formalism. To begin with an informal emphasis on resolution of problems, not documentation and legalism, is felt to be the best base for strong complaint processing productivity and acceptance (a humanizing people-first approach).

This would lead naturally to selection of troubleshooters who resist keeping formal reports and/or extensive transcripts of conversations, notes, persons interviewed, and data sources collected for each of the complaints. Some of the complaint programs examined in the public and private sectors do use extensive documentation as a basis for their work. In this planning group's view, they were considered to be bureaucratic in nature and not much better than the legalistic systems they are designed to be an alternative to.

6. *Confidentiality.* All complaints and complaint responses are to be absolutely confidential. The only qualifying clause was the "duty to warn" in the event of threatened harm by a complainant to another person in the corporation. For example, there would be a duty on the troubleshooter's part to warn a potential victim if someone threatened to murder a supervisor and named the supervisor, time, and place. In the legal literature there is generally an established precedent now that the listener, whether he or she is a counselor or psychiatrist (or probably a troubleshooter), has a duty to warn the target about the impending danger (for example, see Annas, Glantz, and Katz, 1981).

7. *Feedback.* The questions related to confidentiality and the extent of documentation and written reports also involve consideration of how much information is fed back, to whom, why, when, and how. What is reported about a sexual harassment case? The primary feedback goes to the complainant, since this person has a need to know about the outcome of the problem. This should occur very soon after the resolution of the problem, within hours or days (constrained somewhat by the work schedule). When the committee reviewed some of the complaint program designs in existence, they found that they were on a continuum with regard to feedback. Some programs provide

extensive information on the outcome of the problem; others simply tell the complainant that it was solved. There was a split within the planning committee about how this feedback would be given, whether in person or in writing. In keeping with the push for informality, the general belief was that the feedback should be given orally, with no written feedback. Had the committee decided that the pen- and paper-type system would be recommended, there would have to be a written letter documenting the resolution of the complaint.

8. *Data Use*. The design group recommends that some statistics regarding the nature and number of the complaints be kept and that these be passed on to top management. The troubleshooter would develop simple frequency counts, complaints by month, and complaints according to a categorization (of types of complaints). They would not be detailed in any way that could lead to identification of the specific complainants who filed them. There was some vigorous debate about tracking complaints to individual units (departments, divisions, floors), although this was seen as quite valuable to the organization developmentally. Some felt it allows identification of the complainant in highly unique and sensitive complaints. However, units would be able to use the data to spot organization and management problems if they could receive the data in the aggregate, protecting confidentiality.

This memo outlined the technical work system of the troubleshooter program, focusing on eight design elements: target group, primary duties, allowable topics, problem resolution techniques, degree of formality, confidentiality, feedback, and data use. This work system is embedded in a structure that is a combination of the arrangement of the troubleshooter program parts and the whole organizational context. Planning group discussions and decisions about structure are summarized next.

Structural Issues   The planning committee addressed eight structural aspects of the troubleshooter program design, including standardization, specialization, formalization, complexity, centralization, personnel configuration, professionalism, and authority (Daft, 1983; Ziegenfuss, 1985a). All of these are briefly discussed as they would be presented in a planning document developed by the troubleshooter program group.

1. *Standardization.* It was quickly recognized that the trouble-shooter's complaint-taking process and certainly the responses could *not* be standardized. Each complaint is viewed as an individual situation that should be dealt with individually, leaving much space for innovation and creativity. There was considerable concern that the troubleshooter should not be confronted with bureaucratic attempts to standardize the process at the outset of development. How, for example, would one standardize sabotage, transfer, or sexual harassment cases? Facts and outcomes in all cases will be unique. Process and procedures, however, could be specified in somewhat standard-ized fashion.

2. *Specialization.* Should the troubleshooter become a *specialist* in certain types of complaints, for example, in discrimination, hiring/firing, harassment, policy, or promotion issues? The design intent was that the work structure be broad and encompassing, with specialization left to other units (such as the employee assistance program or EEO office) as required. This program was to be a generalist-type problem-solving effort. Troubleshooter work should be diverse and broad, not constrained or directed at only certain types of problems.

3. *Formalization.* How formal should the structure of the pro-gram be? It was agreed that there should be formal recognition from the chief executive officer, appearance on the organiza-tional chart, and inclusion in formal news releases and information memorandums within the organization. These would be evidence of the formal presence of the program. However, as already discussed, the work emphasis is on informal problem solving. The differentiation is between formal recognition of the program in the structure versus formal bureaucratized demands on the problem-solving process. The design group was clearly in favor of a formalized presence in the structure but with wide latitude for informal problem solving, which they believed would be more effective over time.

4. *Complexity.* A clear concern for controlling the potential complexity emerged. The planning group felt that the structure of the program should be "light," "informal," and low in complexity. There were design committee members familiar with legalistic approaches to problem solving, such as arbitration, hearings, and appeals. Their view was that a troubleshooter program is an alternative to complex legalistic systems. Troubleshooters are most effective if the level of complexity is kept to a minimum. This translates often to a design push for informality, as previously discussed. Specifically, forms and reporting and feedback mechanisms are all kept simple and direct.

5. *Centralization.* Should the program be centralized? The program was to be initiated in one of the five divisions of the corporation. If all divisions eventually have a troubleshooter, how will control be maintained? For example, how will a number of hospital troubleshooters in a multihospital system be structured? Should all of the troubleshooters be under centralized control or should the function be decentralized with significant autonomy?

   The planning committee favored decentralization, with each troubleshooter having individual autonomy and freedom. Obviously, there is a need for them to network for support, and to combine data, for example, on the nature and volume of complaints. However, it was felt that strong centralized control would push the program toward formalization, legalization, and bureaucratization, thereby diminishing its effectiveness.

6. *Personnel configuration.* The sixth structural concern translated into a discussion of the type, background, and selection of the troubleshooters. It was decided that the type of person was more important than his or her particular training, whether in human relations, counseling, social work, law, or some other field. There was general agreement that the person should come with very high references as a problem solver. There would be less reliance on specific background training and experience in the corporation, with greater emphasis on personal characteristics. However, the planning group did note

that troubleshooters are not likely to do very well if they are very young or very new in the corporation.

7. *Professionalism.* One of the committee members asked whether or not there was a professional society of troubleshooters. With a bit of digging, it was discovered that there was no such association or organization, but that there was a set of guiding ethics from several related groups such as the Society for Professionals in Dispute Resolution and the Corporate Ombudsman Association. The latter was directly applicable. The troubleshooter would be encouraged to be a member of these societies (for example, adopting their ethics guidelines), particularly if he or she did not come from some field with already established standards, such as psychology or social work. Guidance from members in an established field was thought to assist professional demeanor and actions.

8. *Authority.* The structural question of authority was addressed and here again, the interest of the committee was that significant authority be vested in the troubleshooter, a level of authority that would make it possible to respond to and resolve the most significant complaints. Without this, the troubleshooter will be neutralized, lost in the bureaucracy, identified as a paper shuffler or a public relations flunky for "higher-ups."

These structural suggestions became design guidelines for program development. Some of them raised psychological issues.

Psychosocial Issues Design attention turned next to the acceptance and feelings of the corporate members. The complaint program itself has a "psychosocial" component. The group felt it was necessary to consider how individuals and groups of employees would react to the troubleshooter program; for example, what are their attitudes toward such a program? In their review, the planning group considered six areas: expectations, attitudes, commitment, communication, intergroup conflict, and resistance. This material is presented in summarized form.

1. *Expectations.* With regard to expectations, the planning group felt it was necessary to ensure that employees knew how the

program was to work. New programs of any sort can create considerable anxiety. There was concern that employee anxiety be minimized in the start-up process. This meant providing potential complainants with as much information as possible on how the program would work and on its expected benefits for the organization as a whole and for individual employees. The nature of a troubleshooter program means that addressing expectations is critical.

2. *Attitudes.* What will be the attitudes of the employees toward the new troubleshooter program? Will they be suspicious of the rationale and/or the use of the complaint data? Will they be concerned that it is more a public relations exercise than a real problem-solving mechanism? A particularly important question is how managers will feel about it. Will they be afraid of what the number of complaints will mean to their department and how they will be treated by the senior executive group? In short, the design group felt it was critical to communicate the philosophy of the program (an organization development/ helping intention) to potential users and to lower and middle management so that they would accept it as an effort to improve the quality of work life.

3. *Commitment.* How will employees develop commitment to the program? Fully informing and educating them at the outset would contribute to this commitment. But the design group felt that real commitment would emerge only as a result of the use of the troubleshooter program. The "seeing is believing" notion would be the determinant. If initial complaints are handled fairly, professionally, and with behaviors that actually provided help—not with a policing or an adversarial approach—support would be forthcoming. Policing and the resulting adversarial relations would be capable of killing the program in weeks.

4. *Communication.* The communications concern of the planning group focused on how the purpose, process, and outcome of the complaint program was to be communicated to the organization's members at large. It was decided that a series of memorandums and in-person small group meetings would be held with both managers and employees. The memorandum as

a process for communicating organizational change was not thought to be terribly effective. The in-person sessions between some leading members of the design group and later the troubleshooter would be used to communicate firsthand the purposes and workings of the program. Additionally, this would give the troubleshooter the opportunity to meet the people and to begin to develop relationships.

5. *Intergroup Conflict.* There was some concern that the introduction of the troubleshooter would produce group conflict among groups already offering complaint resolution services. The design group took special care to involve these people (employee assistance program staff, affirmative action, personnel) in the design work and felt that the potential for intergroup conflict was minimal.

6. *Resistance.* The last area of concern was resistance to the program. The design group felt that if all the above steps were carried out appropriately, resistance would be minimized. However, there was some concern that any resistance that got going would be detrimental to the program. Special care should be taken to monitor the acceptance of the program during the first few months of its existence.

These six areas recognize the importance of the psychological side of program design and development. Management has the entire responsibility for these aspects and more.

Managerial Issues   The final topic of concern to the planning group was the management of the new complaint program. Discussion focused on five topics: planning, organizing, developing, directing/leading, and controlling. All of these issues were felt to be critical to the ultimate success of the program. That is, the troubleshooter program must be managed just like any other program in the organization.

1. *Planning.* The planning group was aware that its initial work was essentially strategic in nature. That is, it focused primarily on mission, goals and objectives, and design at a fairly abstract level (Ackoff, 1981; Steiner, 1979; Below, Morrisey, and Acomb,

1987). It was recognized that detailed operational planning would start when the troubleshooter was appointed. He or she would lead the operational planning process. The planning initiated with this design work could continue with the design group as an advisory board. Membership could also involve related persons such as the Equal Employment Opportunity representative and the employee assistance program director.

2. *Organizing.* Creation of the program management structure is done by the troubleshooter. The process could begin with an analysis of the troubleshooter program structures that exist in other organizations, continuing the work of the design group. This could also include visitations to existing programs, for example, at Control Data, IBM, American Express, Digital Equipment, and Anheuser-Busch. Since the "program" is small—one person—there is not an extensive organizing requirement. However, one area of concern was that the information system be developed fairly quickly. It is critical that the information system design be thought through well enough to ensure that the initial complaints become part of future data analysis.

3. *Developing.* "Developing" activities would involve both the program and the individual. Before seeing the pool of candidates, it was not possible to assume that the troubleshooter would have extensive experience. With or without experience, he or she could benefit from exposure to other troubleshooters and to training programs in negotiation and dispute resolution. The troubleshooter was expected to design a one-year self-development plan that included a mix of visitations to other programs, readings of relevant books and papers, and participation in three workshops.

On the program level, the troubleshooter design group agreed to initiate a series of quarterly reviews to identify developmental needs useful to continuing the progress of the program. This developmental review would include a consideration of whether goals and objectives were on target; an analysis of resources required; and a review of the start-up process, specifically targeting those topics that will need attention, such as employee and manager acceptance.

4. *Directing/Leading.* Who will direct the program; that is, who will be responsible for the troubleshooter? There was some question here about the reporting relationship, as discussed earlier. It was decided that direction should come from the chief executive officer of the corporation. This would enable the authority/power linkage to be maximized, providing the direction and leadership necessary to ensure that the trouble-shooter program is an integrated component of an overall organization development strategy.

5. *Controlling.* Control of the program is defined through a series of control guidelines (see Chapter Nine). The design group in an advisory capacity and the CEO would be responsible for initial reviews. As noted in the development section, these reviews would occur quarterly at the outset to ensure that the program was on track.

Management of the troubleshooter program is fairly simple and straightforward, a two-person job involving the troubleshooter and his/her superior. Since there is not an extensive staff or program, the control and management are personal and highly visible. Still, an evaluation following start-up step 4 is useful, as noted in step 5.

Step 4: Start Up and Operate

There is not much to discuss about start-up. This is the "do it" stage. One cautionary note seems appropriate. Troubleshooters need some luck and an inclination to delay confronting the "most major" conflict in the first six months. Until presence and credibility are established, attacking a high-visibility, politically involved problem could cause the program to be killed. An example might be the suspected fudging of sales performance figures by the division sales manager who was personally hired by the CEO. It is better to collect additional data and absolutely secure the position before initiating a review requiring a full-scale test of acceptance and power.

Step 5: Periodically Evaluate Progress

This step calls for a periodic review of the progress of the troubleshooter program. The design group felt that no design was perfect and that periodic adaptations are necessary. A review would need to include level of effort, documentation of case types, frequencies and outcomes, and some inquiry as to how managers and employees feel about the program. Chapter Ten presents the issues to be addressed in examining troubleshooter impact.

The preceding review of formal program start-up should illustrate that a troubleshooter program can be systematically planned and developed, like any other program or product. History, environment, internal host organization characteristics, and the program design itself must be considered.

However, the formal path is only one route to program design and start-up. Many programs begin with an informal effort initiated by an employee or a customer representative, or someone else with a deep interest in solving problems.

The Informal Approach

There is no "standard" way to report an informal start-up. An employee with a real commitment to productivity and work life quality, or with dedication to excellence in customer service, will "drift" into a troubleshooter role. It is happening more and more all the time. Hospitals provide one common example. Patient representatives have been around for some fifteen to twenty years now (Hogan, 1980). There are approximately 3,000 patient representatives (troubleshooters) in hospitals across the United States (AHA Patient Representative Society, personal communication, Dec. 1986 and Nov. 1987). More and more of them are defining themselves as troubleshooters and ombudsmen.

Many patient representatives were hired to assist with public relations; in fact, some even worked in or for the public relations unit. Their job was to help keep the hospital image clean and tidy. Smooth the problems, pacify angry patients, placate egotistical physicians, they were told. They were not directed to engage in real problem solving, work that would involve clinical and management staff confrontation and change. Some hospitals were afraid to; others did not have the idea of problem solving and organizational development as a program concept. Nevertheless, many patient representatives from the first saw themselves as troubleshooters, as ombudsmen for both patients and hospital. Informally, they attempted to use their individual cases and their knowledge of the hospital to achieve change. They became highly skilled at conflict resolution involving angry patients, aloof physicians, and management that was caught in the middle. Troubleshooting patient representatives have been hampered by several barriers, however: (1) a lack of recognition of their true role, (2) a low-level reporting relationship without access to power and authority, and (3) poor data system backup that would enable them to fully document the problems and the problem patterns they encounter.

As "informal troubleshooters," they follow the general work activity plan outlined in Chapter Three, and they work with a wide range of complaints that take them through all parts of the organization. Their work—informal as it is—is widely underrecognized. That will change as their contribution becomes better known, that is, as executives begin to recognize their help in solving difficult problems and in avoiding litigation.

Summary

In this chapter, we considered how the troubleshooter program emerged as a viable entity in one organization. We followed the planning of a formal program through a historical and environmental analysis that considered the kinds of trends that led the organization to develop such a program.

A review of the internal characteristics of the corporation then analyzed the degree to which the troubleshooter concept fit the organization. The topics surveyed included employee characteristics, occupations, power and interest groups, organizational characteristics in general, and the corporation's trends and financial status.

The planning and design group presented their findings regarding the feasibility of introducing the program to the corporation. These considerations involved goals and values, technical aspects of the complaint work, structural design issues, psychological and social issues, and the management of the program. Each of these areas was briefly reviewed with regard to planning considerations.

After a few comments about start-up and evaluation, we turned to the subject of informal programs. An illustrative group of informal troubleshooters—patient representatives—was discussed. The emergence of their troubleshooting/ombudsman role has been gradual over the past fifteen to twenty years. They are formally recognized in their organization, but their work in organization development is informal and unrecognized. No standard plan for internal program start-up is apparent.

In this chapter, in short, we focused on one design and planning experience, the development of a troubleshooter program in a corporation. We now need to hear in some depth about the authority and power of troubleshooters, the kinds of cases they encounter, and how their performance is controlled.

5

Using Authority and Power: Tools for Effective Problem Solving

Introduction

In this chapter, the sources of the troubleshooter's authority and power are examined. The position of the troubleshooter in the organization and the amount of his or her power—the ability to get things done, to solve problems—is reviewed. Authority and power are linked (Kast and Rosenzweig, 1985; Daft, 1983), and it is their convergence that enables the complaints to be resolved and the organization to be developed. Consider the following example:

Firing with Due Compensation

A real estate salesman working on a commercial property sale for nearly a year was fired just before the sale was completed. He protested to the company that he was still due his commission since he put the package together and worked extensively on the project. In a brief telephone call, the company division manager refused his request and afterward would not return telephone messages. The former salesman sued the company.

How would the troubleshooter become engaged in the salesman's commission problem without some level of authority? Where does the power to initiate change come from?

Authority

The management literature includes well-known definitions of types of authority (Max Weber's original view, 1947; Kast and Rosenzweig, 1985, p. 368). Although a bit "ancient," these major types are known by many managers, and most important, they are understandable in a commonsense way. Professional authority is added to Weber's original set of charismatic, traditional, and rational/legal forms of authority. They are noted here as authority sources that converge to become the total authority base for troubleshooters (see Figure 5). Each of these authority sources is reviewed with an example.

Authority Source 1: Charismatic Authority   The first source of a troubleshooter's authority is charismatic authority. The troubleshooter's personal traits and attributes determine in part how much authority he or she has as a complaint taker and problem solver. This authority source differs from the others in that it is based on the personal characteristics of the person in the trouble-shooting job (Weber, 1947; Kast and Rosenzweig, 1985). Each troubleshooter has a different level of charismatic authority. Different levels of charisma are functions of traits such as personal and social likes and dislikes, interpersonal relationship skills, and abilities to negotiate, to be diplomatic, and to be assertive and persistent.

Consider the chapter's opening case, for example. When the troubleshooter is called into the saleman's commission problem, how is he or she regarded? The participants immediately relate to the troubleshooter's traits—will this person listen, be fair, be creative in finding a solution, is he or she a bureaucrat, and so forth? If negative images come to mind based on the troubleshooter's personal traits and demeanor, the charismatic authority level of the troubleshooter will be low. If personal traits produce an image of charisma in the mind of the real estate salesman and his division manager, charismatic authority will be high.

For the author, this is the most important source of authority for the troubleshooter. This authority is not based on formal organizational position (people in certain positions have authority

Figure 5. Sources of Troubleshooters' Authority.

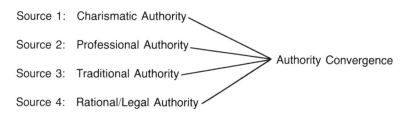

because of that position), but on character traits, interpersonal abilities, and style. Charismatic authority is derived from the behavioral and interpersonal history of the troubleshooter in the organization, particularly if there is a long employment history, for example, as vice president for personnel, or as executive assistant to a senior person. This is because troubleshooters with long tenure in the company have had the opportunity to develop personal sources of support. Troubleshooters who are charismatic establish people linkages that provide support for themselves and their activities (such as problem solving and negotiation of difficult conflicts).

If the troubleshooter does not have personality characteristics suitable to the job—for example, fairness, sincerity, trustworthiness, persistence, and determination—the other sources of authority (professional, traditional, and rational/legal) are significantly undermined, if not totally useless. They will not add much authority to a base of "charismatic deficiency." When a patient ombudsman arranges a meeting to solve a doctor/patient conflict, the physician will only make sincere problem-solving efforts if the ombudsman's credibility is well established. Credibility depends first on personal characteristics, then on other sources of authority.

There is no real separation of a troubleshooter's charismatic authority source from traditional, rational/legal, or professional authority sources. Many troubleshooters recognize that ability to work effectively with complainants, subjects of complaints, and "innocent bystanders" is determined to a large extent by personal credibility. A patient ombudsman colleague with very strong charismatic authority has been investigating complaints for more than eleven years, the last six years in a hospital. Her charismatic authority is based on her unique set of personal characteristics, which I would list as important to all troubleshooters: warmth, determination, fairness, sincerity, ability to listen, assertiveness, and an outgoing personality. When this patient ombudsman arrives on a unit, she is greeted as a warm, supportive problem solver who will fairly and sincerely attempt to solve a problem. There is little or no doubt that the problem *will* be confronted and resolved, no matter how much time is required. That image communicated fully to employees and consumers provides the basis for her charismatic authority. But she also depends on additional authority sources.

Authority Source 2: Professional Authority The second authority source for troubleshooting is professional authority, the troubleshooter's standing in the organization as a professional problem solver. It is derived from the troubleshooter's ability to satisfy the criteria for professionalism, including

- knowledge about problem-solving techniques and theory
- official sanction of the troubleshooter's role nationally, regionally, organizationally
- ethical behavior in terms of confidentiality and fair treatment
- both training and experience in problem solving and complaint taking

The professional authority of a troubleshooter is based on the extent to which he or she is a professional with regard to complaint-taking/problem-solving, education, and consultation actions. Professional demeanor and behavior must be recognized by members of the organization.

Belief in the professionalism of troubleshooting activities is based only in part on formal training and public recognition. Troubleshooters themselves do not yet agree that they have a distinct professional identity. Currently, formal societies and associations for troubleshooters are limited (organizations include the Corporate Ombudsman Association, Patient Representative Society, and Society for Professionals in Dispute Resolution). There are, for example, no schools of ombudsman training. The professionalism is based more on a connection with allied fields such as dispute resolution, negotiation, industrial relations, arbitration, law, psychology, and organizational behavior and development. Each of these fields has a set of generally accepted principles, behaviors bounded by ethical constraints and expectations for the role of persons who identify themselves with the field (the traditional aspects of professionalism; Vollmer and Mills, 1966). To the extent that troubleshooting is similar and/or identical to work in other fields (for example, psychology, labor law), the professional authority base is established and developed over time by the connections with that field. A troubleshooter who is a professionally trained labor negotiator has the benefit of the recognition, guidance, and support of the people and practices in that field.

Some ombudsmen are trained industrial psychologists (at the Ph.D. level). When they come into a unit as official troubleshooter, staff recognize their credentials, including the expertise and ethics and the weight of the profession. The total of all of the implied elements of professionalism creates the authority. Others are faculty, nurses, and engineers with similar professional roots.

Troubleshooters without this identifiable connection to a professional field build an image of professionalism based on their behavior and knowledge. Executive assistants or former managers will be recognized in time as having authority that derives from their professional manner of problem solving even though they may not ever be identified with a "professional" problem-solving field.

Authority Source 3: Traditional Authority   The third source of troubleshooter authority is tradition. Authority through tradition (Weber, 1947; Kast and Rosenzweig, 1985) is established only by troubleshooters who are in operation over a long period of time—several years or more. After five to eight years of successful work, the program is accepted by the organizational culture. Acceptance means that complaint taking, problem solving, and the troubleshooter approach to enhancing productivity have become part of the "tradition" of the corporation or public agency. Company tradition says that the troubleshooter has recognized authority to mediate conflicts, assist in removing barriers to productivity, and generally promote the quality of working life through open communication.

In one hospital ombudsman program, it took about five years for the patient ombudsman to develop the tradition of problem confrontation and problem solving. Part of the time requirement was due to the years needed to generate complaints hospitalwide. Tradition had to be developed from ombudsman experience in all units of the hospital. Secondhand experience— comment from colleagues who dealt with the ombudsman—is also necessary but is not sufficient for full tradition building.

There is one way to develop this "traditional authority" without waiting for the years of official troubleshooter experience. When considering candidates for the position of troubleshooter (a newly established formal position), select an employee who has had both wide experience in the organization and who throughout that experience has established his or her own personal tradition of problem solving, fair play, and productive actions. This is an approach to selection that is based on the assumption that all organizations now have troubleshooters but do not officially recognize them!

At least one corporate ombudsman program at a large bank uses this mechanism to assist in establishing the authority base (Tillier, 1987). A career senior executive is chosen to be ombudsman for the final years prior to retirement. Traditional and charismatic authority are linked—the person chosen has strong personal characteristics and a successful corporate history. Authority is established by the tradition of performance and the confidence vested in that executive over decades.

Consider again the case of the salesman's commission. Contrast the reception given to a troubleshooter who was a relatively new employee of the company (less than five years) with that of a senior executive with a long and successful corporate history. Common sense indicates that the senior official would begin with higher levels of authority. The organization trades on the personal history of the individual to begin to establish a troubleshooting tradition.

There is a fourth authority source derived from relations with the law.

Authority Source 4: Rational/Legal Authority The fourth
source of troubleshooter authority is rational/legal authority
derived from the troubleshooter's function as a quasi-legal
interpreter (Weber, 1947; Kast and Rosenzweig, 1985). The troubleshooter interprets/explains/teaches the official rules and regulations of the organization—policies and procedures—as well as the
practical implications of internal (individual and group behavior)
and external (industrywide) perceptions and pressures. The
complaints that arise in the organization are often related to or
directly involve quasi-legal issues. For example, many patient
complaints could have medical malpractice implications. This
authority base is founded on the need to ensure that official policies
and procedures are the guidelines for employees' behaviors.

With regard to the salesman's commission case, what is the
organization's official position on payment to a former employee?
If there are written policies, they may only need to be shared with
the complainant. Is there a need for a formal legal opinion about
whether the employee is owed the commission? If uncertainty exists,
the troubleshooter can assist the organization in making the
decision, including concern for precedent.

Organizations operate somewhat rationally, guided by a set
of policy and procedural guidelines that determine the acceptable
behaviors of organizational members, or at least the boundaries of
behavior. As interpreters of official rules, troubleshooters have
rational/legal authority to resolve conflicts and complaints. Does a
hospital patient have a right to be informed about the purpose,
process, and benefits of a given medical treatment? The physician
may be resisting informed consent, but by law and by the hospital's
medical policy (which the physican forgot about), the patient must
be told. The authority is rational/legal, backed by the full weight
of the organization.

This authority from the troubleshooter's position in the
organization and the official rules and regulations are used to help
guide consumer and employee behaviors. Prescribing behavior via
rules does not fit very well with what we know about how
organizations work. Employees do not behave according to a set of
rules. Rule and policy interpretation helps to establish a base for
problem-solving actions. Many employees and consumers relate

only to the "enforced authority" of official policies, changing their behaviors only when regulations and laws are cited. Some physicians may not voluntarily inform a patient about treatment in response to a request, but they would provide information in compliance with the law. The troubleshooter uses this authority when applicable to the participants and the case.

The primary authority source used by troubleshooters is likely to be different, based on their individual differences. Some rely more on their charisma, others on their professionalism. It is the total constellation of authority sources that creates the authority base for the troubleshooter programs. This authority base remains intact when a troubleshooter leaves, but a new troubleshooter may switch the primary source of authority from charismatic, for example, to professional. Traditional authority will increase as the "tradition" of troubleshooting flourishes in an organization (over time with different people).

All troubleshooters need power to encourage and to ensure the changes that effectively resolve problems.

Power

Power is the ability to get things done. As with authority, there is no single source of power. One commentator offered a set of six sources that troubleshooters rely on to generate "action abilities" within the organization (Filley, House, and Kerr, 1976; also see Ziegenfuss, 1985c). As in the case of authority, these six sources converge to create a power base (see Figure 6). The convergence of diverse power sources produces the ability of the troubleshooter to achieve problem-solving and organizational development objectives. Just as troubleshooters draw on different sources of authority according to who they are as individuals and according to the needs of the situation, power to initiate change comes from a similar set of sources. The whole set of power elements accounts for the level of the troubleshooters' power. They draw on one or more power sources according to the situation they are in and the people involved in the case. A brief explanation of each power source identifies the nature of this action ability.

Figure 6. Sources of Troubleshooters' Power.

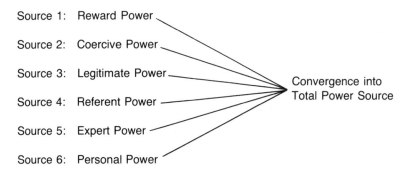

Source 1:   Reward Power

Source 2:   Coercive Power

Source 3:   Legitimate Power

Source 4:   Referent Power

Source 5:   Expert Power

Source 6:   Personal Power

Convergence into
Total Power Source

Power Source 1: Reward Power   Reward power is often the first noticed by managers and employees. It is one of four sources of troubleshooters' power representing the organization's dominant influence on its members. Reward power derives from the ability of the chief executive officer to distribute rewards to those employees who are productive and punishments to those who are not (Filley and Grimes, 1967; Filley, House, and Kerr, 1976; Ziegenfuss, 1985c). Troubleshooters know that there is widespread recognition and some fear that the number of complaints in one's department can negatively affect the extent of the rewards one receives (promotions, bonus, additional staff). How many division managers will receive bonuses after firing a series of salespeople who sue?

The reward power of troubleshooters is based on the realization that a list of complaint topics with frequencies may affect the rewards that an executive or department director receives, such as compensation, access to capital, or staff support. In talking to an executive or other employee about the need to solve a problem or to negotiate a conflict, troubleshooters directly or indirectly imply that a refusal to engage in the problem-solving process may affect future rewards, personal and/or departmental.

Use of a direct threat to deny rewards will negate the acceptance of troubleshooters and turn the program into a police action. Few troubleshooters do that. But the possibility is always present.

An example of this is the case of the hospital admissions department director. The admissions department director was interested in promotion to a higher level of management within the hospital. But there were a large number of complaints in the department about the scheduling of work, errors on admissions forms, and conflicts with other units. When a patient complained about unnecessary admission delay, the patient ombudsman was confident about a sincere attempt to respond when she presented the complaints. She knew that the fear of losing the desired promotion would motivate the admissions director to solve the problem. This did not have to be mentioned directly, at least not to this manager. Complaint levels and managerial willingness to respond are indicators of managerial effectiveness. While the ombudsman does not control the reward system, the close relationship with senior management guarantees her input to decision making.

Power Source 2: Coercive Power Coercive power is the second power source for troubleshooters. It relates directly to the threat inherent in a request to negotiate a solution to a conflict (Filley and Grimes, 1967; Filley, House, and Kerr, 1976; Ziegenfuss, 1985c). Troubleshooters arrive at the conflict situation with an ability to force change if necessary. Under somewhat ideal circumstances, all employees and consumers realize that troubleshooters are sanctioned by the organization, supported by the chief executive, and have top management's coerceive power behind them (although it may not be used often). For example, one corporate ombudsman had difficulty getting two managers to meet in order to solve a personality conflict involving a sales and a production unit. In an attempt to resolve the stalemate, the troubleshooter referred to his ability to coerce a solution by drawing on his relationship with the chief executive. The managers agreed to meet.

It is important to recognize that coercive power is not an effective means for solving many problems, or for solving even a few problems over a long period of time. When employees are forced to change, they tend to do so without commitment, lacking the persistence required for follow-through. The coercive power base exists more often as an implied threat that is not put to use by troubleshooters, at least not by the good ones. As with reward power, coercive power is always there but is rarely used.

There are, however, some managers and employees who will

not respond to anything but coercive power. Whether by training, experience, or personal preference, they relate only to authority-backed commands.

   Power Source 3: Legitimate Power   Legitimate power is the third power source in this connected set. It is based on the troubleshooter's sanction by the organization, including recognition by the chief executive and senior management that the troubleshooter is "a legitimate part of the organization" (Filley and Grimes, 1967; Filley, House, and Kerr, 1976; Ziegenfuss, 1985c). This power tends to come "on line" only after some period of operation, during which the troubleshooter concept and the person in the role demonstrate performance sufficient to convince senior management of their value. An important point here is that troubleshooters are not outside resources coming in on an informal or infrequent occasion to lend a hand. They are a recognized and official source of problem solving within the organization. When legitimacy is established, the troubleshooter has a standing similar to the corporate legal office, the Equal Employment Opportunity office, and the staff units that work to improve organizational process and functioning (for example, personnel, planning). The legitimizing of the function occurs through placement in the organization with reporting responsibilities to a high executive. Promotion of the function within the organization creates a power source based on legitimate recognition.

   This legitimizing can be done with the help of titles, office placement, salary, and meeting access. One corporate ombudsman is special assistant to the president (title). A patient ombudsman's office is located on the first floor of the hospital with high lobby visibility (placement). Some corporate ombudsmen are well paid ($80,000 to $120,000), while others are allowed to attend any and all meetings they feel are relevant to their troubleshooting work (access). One international bank's ombudsman is a senior career executive (World Bank) (history). One airline troubleshooter is a senior manager who also represents the company to government agencies (Air Canada) (representation). All these are "legitimizing" factors that produce power.

Power Source 4: Referent Power   The fourth source of power in the troubleshooting job is referent power. This is the power of the troubleshooter derived from the chief executive officer or senior manager to whom he or she reports (Filley and Grimes, 1967; Filley, House, and Kerr, 1976; Ziegenfuss, 1985c). Quite simply, this means that the troubleshooter achieves some significant degree of power through his or her relationship with the senior manager. If the executive is powerful, that power will "spin off" to the troubleshooter.

For example, in one company the corporate ombudsman reports to the senior vice president for human relations, who has a well-established track record for successfully promoting both productivity and employee quality of working life. The vice president had a hand in selecting the ombudsman for the position and was very active in informing employees and management of the purposes, work activities, and expected benefits of the ombudsman's work. The senior vice president was instrumental in beginning to establish the power base for the company troubleshooter. Those employees and managers who would not initially acknowledge the ombudsman's power *would* recognize that he reports to the senior vice president, who has thirty-five years in the corporation and many connections.

Troubleshooter referent power depends on a combination of the position and personal characteristics of the supervisor. Unfortunately, some troubleshooters report to persons who are not powerful in their organizations, as in the case of a patient ombudsman who reports to the social work department director. The patient troubleshooter's referent power is significantly diminished because it is dependent on a unit that has limited power, a director lower in status and prestige in the medical pecking order.

These four types of power sources—reward, coercive, legitimate, and referent—relate to the organization and are derived from it. To a great extent, the troubleshooter does not have much control over these sources of his or her own power. Rewards are given out by the chief executive officer. The degree to which both the troubleshooter and senior management want to be coercive is determined largely by that manager's group. Whether or not the troubleshooter is legitimate is determined by the status given the troubleshooting function in the organization. Finally, the referent power generated by referral to the reporting senior manager is outside the control of the troubleshooter as well.

Two other power sources—expert power and personal power—are related to the troubleshooter personally. That is, troubleshooters can develop expertise *and* they have a certain set of personal characteristics that comprise their personal power base.

Power Source 5: Expert Power   Expert power is based on the amount of expertise the troubleshooter has developed (Filley and Grimes, 1967; Filley, House, and Kerr, 1976; Ziegenfuss, 1985c). Expertise in this job pertains specifically to the three main troubleshooting activities, including complaint processing, education and training, and consultation. Expert power is derived from the troubleshooter's ability to fulfill these core functions of the job.

This type of power is visible to employees and consumers as they watch the troubleshooter in action. Expert power does not derive from personal style but from the level of technical skill. Conflict participants—employees and managers—ask themselves:

- Is the troubleshooter a good negotiator?
- Is the troubleshooter a conflict resolution expert?
- Is the troubleshooter an effective listener and teacher?
- Does the troubleshooter generate effective and lasting solutions?

When the answer to these questions is yes, this data is added to knowledge of the troubleshooter's character, training, and experience to create a judgment about the level of expert power.

Power Source 6: Personal Power   The final source of power for the troubleshooter is personal power (Filley and Grimes, 1967; Filley, House, and Kerr, 1976; Ziegenfuss, 1985c). This is power developed as a result of the individual traits and characteristics of the troubleshooter. It is how troubleshooters interact with people on a day-to-day basis; whether they are able to resolve problems in a fair and equitable way; whether they relate to conflicts with objectivity, determination, and openness; and whether they have an ability to appreciate the goals and values of individuals, of individual units, and of the organization as a whole. Here again the personnel characteristics defined in the discussion on charismatic authority are relevant. Does the troubleshooter have sincerity, fairness, interpersonal skills, creativity, and determination? This unique mix of the traits of individual troubleshooters and their behavior over time develops a personal power base that determines whether the troubleshooter will be personally effective within the organization.

Summary

In this chapter, the elements of authority and power of the troubleshooter were presented. They are a diverse set that in combination become the power and authority for the entire troubleshooter role. Authority was defined as a merger of four types: charismatic, professional, traditional, and rational/legal. The four types vary in importance for each troubleshooter.

Power was defined as a derivative of six types: reward, coercive, legitimate, referent, expert, and personal power. These sources also vary by level for each individual troubleshooter.

Both the authority and the power of troubleshooters are related to their information processing and communication work, the topic of Chapter Six.

6

Helping Employees, Managers, and Customers Communicate

From the first publications on troubleshooters, there was strong recognition that troubleshooters are communicators for employees, managers, and consumers. But just how are they useful communicators, for whom and on what topics?

Corporations consistently have problems with employee communication. Even executives rate communication as a leading problem, one they continually struggle with (Kiechel, 1986). Troubleshooters are not the sole answer to the executive communication problem, but they are one significant response, a response more human than mere memos and one-way television. Yet some executives express strong skepticism about the troubleshooter's value as a communication resource, suggesting that it subverts management's communication role. Others feel that using troubleshooters for information violates the confidentiality guidelines that enable them to function.

In response to these concerns, a review of why troubleshooter programs are a communication tool will be helpful. What are the outcomes and benefits of the troubleshooter's role in organizational communications? The following discussion presents the rationale for using troubleshooters to help employees, customers, and management communicate.

Communication and Information System Purposes

How and why is the troubleshooter a communicator? The question concerns the use of information about problems (and successes) in organizations. Weiss suggested that information gatherers and researchers in organizations (including troubleshooters) can provide many benefits. In her view (1981, p. 197) there are three purposes for information in any organization, whether a public agency or private corporation. The first is a warning function: "A first step is to recognize that information—including, but not limited to, research information—can serve three distinct functions for organizations. First, it provides *warning*. It indicates the organization is doing something, or failing to do something, that may incur penalties. Many forms of information can fulfill this function, from phone calls from disgruntled clients, staff griev- ances, or newspaper exposes to program statistics, audit reports, or public opinion polls."

How do these purposes fit with the troubleshooting concept? By taking complaints from customers and employees, the trouble- shooter is a warning system communicating to executives that things are amiss in their organization. The official troubleshooter is a formal "early warning device" by which deficiencies in the organization are exposed through actual complaints (data), not conjecture. Troubleshooters must let people know about problems for at least two reasons: (1) to enhance the overall quality of working life (including individual work situations), and (2) to protect their own and their colleagues' investment in the organiza- tion's productivity and viability. Both employees and customers have a vested interest in the corporation (Mitroff, 1983). By feeding back to management, technical unit leaders, and human resource people data about problems (not the exact problems that would violate a confidence, but the general nature of the difficulties being experienced by organizational members), troubleshooters enable executives to take corrective action before the early warning signs are replaced by major disasters, thereby protecting employees' and customers' interests.

For example, when one patient complains about an ortho- pedic surgeon—his arrogance and less than full disclosure—it may only be an isolated problem. However, a series of complaints not only about that surgeon but about the whole group of orthopedic surgeons indicates that a more significant problem may be developing. These are early warning signs that a troubleshooting patient representative could communicate to management before a major medical malpractice action is taken.

Here is a second example:

Policy Violation

Ralph Hansen was an employee of the brewery for thirty-four years, a shift supervisor for the past fourteen. The brewery allowed beer breaks to all employees at mid-afternoon. The new plant manager was not a beer drinker and he thought the policy inappropriate. He also did not get along with Ralph Hansen. The company decided to abolish the free beer rule and prohibit 3:00 P.M. drinking. During the second week of the new policy, the plant manager caught Mr. Hansen drinking a beer on his own. He abruptly fired him for policy violation.

Has Mr. Hansen brought out a general problem of inadequate policy disclosure? Or does the problem rest entirely with the employee? What needs to be communicated to management about the nature of the beer policy problem?

It is critical to know what problems exist in the organization—the identification of problems is a key first step for all corrective actions—but there are other steps that must be taken before corrective action effects a solution. This leads to the second purpose for information, according to Weiss (1981, p. 198): "A second function of information, including social science information, is *guidance*. It can give direction for improvement in agency activities. Again, most of the information that agencies use to adjust their activities comes from sources other than research and analysis, for example from the experience of practitioners. Nevertheless, research and analysis are also potential sources of guidance . . . thus, research's major contribution is often negative: it demonstrates which activities in the organizational repertoire are ineffective and guides the organization in discarding them, reducing the resources committed to them, or perhaps restructuring them."

How does Weiss's second function of information relate to the troubleshooter as communicator? The second function suggests that identifying the nature of the problems being experienced in the organization (the first function) is necessary but not sufficient. A second step is needed to identify and select the appropriate corrective actions. What kinds of options for response does the organization have as a result of the problems it is experiencing? Should it drop products (for example, no further orthopedic surgery)? Should it change policies and procedures, such as regarding beer breaks? Should it increase or decrease the resources committed to a certain activity such as sensitivity training for customer relations? (Many hospitals have started guest relations training programs.)

For example, in one corporation, there has been a long-standing policy designed to eliminate overuse of sick days. However, as a result of a series of complaints to the troubleshooter by employees, it was discovered that few people (if any, it seemed) knew that the policy existed. This kind of information generated by the troubleshooter through the complaint investigation would be communicated to management and, in turn, lead the organization to a response (at the very least distribution and promotion of the policy). Troubleshooter complaint information and its communication to management is used to identify the type and nature of the response required to correct the problem.

This leads us to the question of whether there should be some formal analysis of the troubleshooting data. Should troubleshooters report only isolated incidents? Should they develop a quarterly or yearly report on the nature, volume, and derivation of complaints in the corporation? How detailed and formal should their communication be?

An answer to this question can cause significant debate during the first and subsequent phases of the development of troubleshooter programs. The debate involves the conflict between the need for the information and the need for absolute confidentiality for the complainants. In a hospital, if management does not know of patient complaints, how can they act? But if physicians can identify the patient complainants, will there be conscious or covert retribution? What about inmates in a prison, or employees in a factory located in a town with high unemployment? How would they be affected if their complaints are known?

A third purpose for complaint information is ambitious and somewhat indirect, involving the culture of the organization as a whole. It is an intangible topic, not quite like receiving complaints from customers about products or from employees about an inadequate condition on the assembly line. The following is Weiss's (1981, p. 199) third information purpose: *"Reorientation.* Research [and troubleshooter data] can provide alternative perspectives for understanding and interpreting events. It can challenge the assumptions that underlie organizational programs and offer new concepts, new ideas, new ways of thinking about issues. For example, it can alter organization members' perceptions of what constitutes a warning to the stability of the organization, and it can create a shift in what is perceived as guidance. By offering new frames of reference, it can help an organization reinterpret what it has been doing and open new vistas for the future. Perhaps above all, it can provoke a willingness to think quickly about the organization—its mission, its goals, its activities, its standards of success. The ideas from social science may be able to stimulate internal self examination, which may often be the best route to organizational renewal."

This last purpose of information is obviously the most challenging. It suggests that bits of information and the analytical communication that the troubleshooter provides to executives are a stimulus for altering perceptions about the nature and performance of the company or agency. How does this happen? Almost everyone in an executive group assumes that they are going in the right direction. A typical self-analysis statement might be: "We're all bright and competitive managers. Our group is a high-performance-oriented, likable, and capable group. We have had nothing but success." But there are alternative perceptions of actions they take and the products they deliver to customers. When high-powered hospital physicians and nurses are "too busy" to spend time listening to patient concerns about their hospital stay, a perceived problem may develop. Physicians and nurses are pressed for productivity, meaning that they need to see as many patients as they can. But patients begin to question whether the technical care they are receiving is as good as it should be. The purely technical aspects of quality may be adequate or absolutely first rate. Technical quality is not the problem. The *perception* of inadequate attention will undermine the assessment of quality in the patient's view. Perceptions that employees have about internal barriers to productivity and perceptions that customers have about poor products or service are examples. Quite obviously, employee and customer perceptions are relevant to a successful business, especially for detecting changes in corporate performance (that is, as indicators of success or failure).

Complaints collected and organized as information present executives with employees' and consumers' perceptions of executive actions. This can be taken negatively, as criticism, or it can be taken as data stimulus for rethinking the culture of the organization, the products and services it is producing, and/or the way it treats employees and customers. As Weiss noted, this is one ingredient for creating organizational renewal. The communication of complaint data by the troubleshooters becomes one information source for the continuing organizational development process that all good organizations have.

These three purposes—warning, guidance, and reorientation—comprise the rationale for the troubleshooters' information gathering and communication activities. Troubleshooters are communicators and are therefore part of the greater management information system that provides both baseline data and change data needed for monitoring organizational performance. Given this rationale, the next question is, how do we set up the information system to support the troubleshooter as communicator? What does the troubleshooter's information system design look like and how would it work?

Information System Design and Operation

A troubleshooter program design group working on a formal program would need to plan in detail the design of the information system. They could proceed through a series of steps used to establish complaint and communication information systems (Ziegenfuss, 1985c). The step series is a diagnosis/planning/action/evaluation cycle well known to organizational development practitioners (Ziegenfuss and Ziegenfuss, 1984). Adapted from complaint information system designs (Ziegenfuss, 1985c), the following steps outline the major topics to be addressed in the design of an information system that will support the communication work of the troubleshooter:

> *Step 1:* Identify users.
> *Step 2:* Identify decision areas.
> *Step 3:* Describe current problem data system.
> *Step 4:* Construct idealized design of new system.
> *Step 5:* Gain agreement on the design.
> *Step 6:* Develop information system design specifications in detail.
> *Step 7:* Specify procedures and operational conditions.

Each of these steps is briefly described. The reader is cautioned that this is the design of a formal information system for a formal troubleshooter program. Few formal information systems exist to support informal troubleshooters not officially recognized by their companies.

As an opening requirement, all steps in the design process must include concern for confidentiality. For example, if an employee were concerned about possible cocaine use by a co-worker, or about a co-worker's possible AIDS virus, what would information release by the troubleshooter accomplish? Without trust in confidentiality, the complaining employee would not seek help. And if information of that sort (AIDS, drug use) is released, great personal and organizational damage is done. If information about a troubleshooter client is given out, any possibility of troubleshooter program acceptance is lost for future clients. This must be taken as a starting assumption inherent in each design step.

Step 1: Identify Users The first step in establishing the troubleshooter's information system is to identify the users of the complaint and problem data. The first and most critical user is the chief executive officer, to whom the troubleshooter reports. There must be a means to ensure that the CEO is a "user" of complaint data. Otherwise, the organizational development purposes that require top management leadership are lost. Without senior management and especially the CEO's knowledge of complaint data, there is no warning, guidance, or reorientation possible at the top of the organization (that is, the three information system purposes are not realized).

The CEO must know that individual complaints about fairness such as the policy violation of Ralph Hansen are addressed. But it is even more important that the CEO know if an organization-wide policy problem is causing distress to the company, or that there are problems with high litigation potential.

The second key user is the vice president for human resources, to whom the troubleshooter may report. This is the manager responsible for troubleshooter work, either directly through supervision or indirectly because the work is often "human troubleshooting." There is a natural need for this vice president to know about the nature of the complaints and the level of the conflict activity because it is his or her work area. The complaints intimately involve human relations within the organization. The vice president for human resources must know and understand the data. This vice president would be expected to respond to the warnings, listen to the suggestions for intervention (guidance), and consider reorientation of the human dynamics of the corporation. Troubleshooters for customer complaints would need the vice president for customer relations and vice presidents of sales and marketing to know the data. In one company, the vice president of customer assurance coordinates responses (Altany, 1987).

Two examples illustrate these points. The case of cheating at the company softball game indicated that the level of competition in employee sports may need to be addressed—a human systems problem. Competition that produces intense cheating is not desirable. The interpersonal dynamics that produced it must be addressed, including the impact on and implications for ethics throughout the company.

As to customers, physician communication is a problem in many hospitals. Unwillingness to talk openly and thoroughly with patients and their families can contribute to a patient inclination to litigate problems. Patients who feel that staff are arrogant and noncommunicative may opt for a dialogue in court. A hospital patient relations vice president must ensure that communication is a valued element of the hospital's corporate culture. When indicators of its absence are brought out in the form of complaints, the vice president must know.

The third main user is the vice president for operations/ production (or similar title). This is the key technical vice president responsible for the primary production work of the organization, such as vice president-engineering, vice president-medical staff, vice president-nursing, dean of the faculty. Since some complaints involve technical processes, it is necessary to have the lead technical people involved as information receivers. Without "problem data," technical chiefs are not knowledgeable about product or service deficiencies. Without warnings about defects, how will they know how to respond? Unit directors of the technical departments are necessary complaint data users too, depending on the nature of the complaints and the location (specific department).

For example, would complaints from Ford Pinto owners have resulted in earlier corrective action? Would comments/ complaints from baby crib owners have produced a technical redesign that increased safety and prevented baby deaths from strangulation? No one can be sure, and perhaps the answer is no. But the point is made—there is a better chance of spotting technical deficiencies if employees and consumers are allowed to voice their complaints with the data flowing to people able to respond.

Finally, specialists in various human resources departments (EEO, employee assistance) would be users of the data as well. They would be particularly interested in the number of complaints that concern their special problem area. And they would need to ensure that the troubleshooter's role as one of the gatekeepers to their system is well established and maintained.

In summary, step 1 identifies key users of troubleshooting data.

Step 2: Identify Decision Areas   Information is communicated to support decisions. What are the decision areas for which complaint data would be helpful? The users define the decision areas. We need to think about who the users are and why they need the information communicated by troubleshooters (Ziegenfuss, 1985c, pp. 171-174).

First, the chief executive needs to know how employees and consumers feel about the direction of the company and its operations. Is the organization on track from a personnel standpoint? Are the goods and services high quality? Are customers happy or angry? Complaints coming from employees about working conditions or from customers about the quality of the products enable the executive to evaluate the company. With significant complaints, managers might be confronted with an alternative view of the culture of the organization or its outputs.

Second, complaints about human relations are critical. The complaint data system is an early warning device for detecting serious or emerging concerns in human commitment, morale, expectations, security, satisfaction, conflict—all mainstream topics of human relations. Information communicated by troubleshooters increases organizational knowledge in human relations. By communicating issues and problems, they are helping the organization learn about itself.

Last, troubleshooting data provides information about the level of technical performance. Do employees feel that they are turning out quality products, ones that are built to last? Or do employees complain about pushing production so hard that shoddiness is the primary result? How do customers feel? Are they satisfied with the goods and services? As noted previously, this data is "needed information" for defining the path to organizational excellence (Peters and Waterman, 1984). Employee and consumer input is critical for evaluating performance and for guiding future action. One company, Westinghouse Furniture, has created a vice president–customer assurance to lead problem solving on customer concerns (Altany, 1987). Complaint data can provide the topics for action.

Step 3: Describe Current Problem Data System   Design involves asking the question, what is the *usual* means for gathering information on culture, human relations, and performance? How do the chief executive officer and the vice presidents for human resources and for operations find out how they are doing? In many organizations, collecting information about the reasons for falling performance and productivity barriers is, at best, a hit-or-miss proposition. Management feedback from participants is often light. Executives rarely hear how things are going because the higher your position is in the organization, the less likely people are to tell you that things are not going well! Additionally, the higher your position in the organization, the more your competence and your performance are *assumed,* as opposed to being tested openly. The Center for Creative Leadership (Kaplan, Drath, and Kofodimos, 1984, p. 7) summarized the power/communication problem with regard to employee complaints quite nicely: "The exercise of power impedes the flow of constructive criticism. Yet power must be exercised if executives are to do their jobs. So the issue is not how to reduce the power the executive needs, but how to manage those aspects of its exercise that impede criticism. The motive to do this will vary with the value that is placed on continuing growth and learning for executives who have already reached the very top. If we see such development as being important for top executives, then getting criticism to executives is a proportionally important problem. For when we know ourselves 'but slenderly,' we face slim odds in our endeavor to develop our fullest capabilities." This quotation indicates that it is very important to get complaint data to top executives, but methods for doing so are frequently deficient or lacking altogether. As a result, the little information that executives do get is informal, disconnected, and unclear as to validity and reliability.

Describing current information systems for complaints is relatively easy—there are few formal systems. *Any* steps a trouble-shooter took in this direction is likely to represent improvement, that is, more information for executives. For example, an executive could monitor the type and nature of complaints after organizational change as one way of obtaining feedback on new ventures. In one hospital recently reorganized as a holding company, there was high interest in new products and subsidiary ventures. A senior vice president for product development was asked to design and put into operation a twenty-four-hour family practice clinic at a nearby mall. After nine months of operation, the president asked the vice president how it was going. Like all "good" vice presidents, he answered, "Absolutely fine, Chief." In the next six months, the president received a series of oral and written communications (complaint data) from the hospital's ombudsman. It turned out that things were not going well at all. Both physicians and patients were complaining about the clinic's operations. The president then asked his vice president the same question, this time with data raising specific questions about *actual* operation. The executive was able to test the glowing self-reports by the vice president. The president did not fire the vice president—an action that would be inconsistent with the purpose of complaint data as an organizational development tool. He did, however, ask for a detailed problem correction plan.

The problem addressed by this complaint data flow is articulately presented by Ackoff in an article that appeared in the *Wharton Alumni Magazine*. He noted (1985, p. 26) that

> There are many ways of facilitating communication upward in hierarchical organizations, for example, suggestion boxes, company newspapers, "open doors," inter-level meetings, and ombudsmen. But state-of-the-organization addresses by a high-ranking official to assembled subordinates is not one of them even if followed by discussion. The presenting superiors usually believe this gives their subordinates ample opportunity to communicate with them. This is seldom the case. Superiors can only hear what their subordinates want to say in meetings arranged and conducted by them. . . .
>
> Subordinates are reluctant to relay upward messages that they believe their superiors would rather not receive, or that reflect negatively on the relayer. The bearer of bad news, even if not its source, is often received badly. This is reflected in the statement attributed to Samuel Goldwyn which was something like, "I want you to say what you think even if I fire you for it." Fear of retribution for criticizing a superior is responsible for the high non-response rates usually obtained in internal attitude surveys. Respondents doubt that the anonymity of their submissions will be preserved and they doubt the willingness of their superiors to face "the truth" about themselves.

The creation of a means of uncovering and confronting problems and the nature of organizational reality is a critical need. Without a strong openness to criticism, the general approach has been to accept limited feedback. "Everything is fine," say almost all vice presidents. The presence of a trusted troubleshooter with highly developed communication skills may be just the strategy needed to help executives overcome this resistance. Over time, the resistance to feedback and to problem confrontation is lowered because of the troubleshooter's style and organizational development intentions.

Step 4: Construct Idealized Design of New System   The next step in the design process is to create an idealized version of the best possible design for the information system at the time. What type of data system will best support troubleshooter communication? This is not idealized in the sense of utopian, but derives from Ackoff's systems thinking and planning. It is the best design that could be established at the time of the start-up of the troubleshooter program (Ackoff, 1981). This design must have three characteristics: (1) it must be technologically feasible, (2) it must be operationally viable, and (3) it must be capable of learning and adaptation in the future (Ackoff, 1981, p. 105). This means that the troubleshooter's information system design must be very basic, that it must be able to be carried out without requiring a staff of nineteen information analysts and $2 million in equipment, and that it be capable of future development. These requirements lead to a simplified design with the following characteristics:

1. Only four types of data are collected: type of complaint, nature of complaint, volume, and location (by department).
2. Reports would be compiled quarterly using only aggregate data.
3. After reports are sent to the users the first two quarters, the users are interviewed for redesign suggestions.
4. The system is redesigned about every six to twelve months, gradually elaborating the coverage and sophistication of the system as needs and use warrants.

This process creates a design/redesign procedure that keeps the system adaptive and growing concurrent with the adaptation and growth of the troubleshooter program as a whole. Information capability and sophistication develop as do the acceptance and capability of the troubleshooter.

Step 5: Gain Agreement on the Design After constructing an initial version of the information system design, it is "floated" to various members of the executive group, to the users and the users' department representatives. There are several reasons for obtaining user feedback. Users will have suggestions about information needs and how they would like to receive data. Two purposes of this step are to generate additional design suggestions and to identify any errors in design thinking. For example, managers need to know whether there are many policy misunderstandings, for instance involving transfer notices, customer return and replacement policies, and so on. If employees do not understand or do not know of new policies or significant policy changes, internal communications must be strengthened.

The discussions with future users are held to stimulate interest in the type of information that managers could receive as a result of the complaint taking and processing. Participation in the data system design process is to build user interest, in a marketing sense. As the information system develops, so does the program. Both are promoted simultaneously as a prelude to forthcoming troubleshooter communications.

Last, meetings with the users are to create support for the information system. The participative design process is to build consensus on the need for troubleshooting information. If no consensus emerges on the need for and the use of this kind of information, there is little reason to develop and distribute reports. They would not be read and the information in them would not be used. This scenario is the one to be avoided beginning at the design point. The consensus-building process is used to educate potential users on the purpose, process, and expected outcomes of data-supported communication from the troubleshooter.

Step 6: Develop Information System Design Specifications in Detail In step 6, the detailed elements of the troubleshooter information system are identified. This means defining the reason why each piece of data would be collected and distributed. The

following are sample elements of one ombudsman's information
system:

- type of complaint (category descriptor)
- nature of complaint
- volume by type
- characteristics of complainant
  —age
  —sex
  —race
  —location
  —occupation
- validity of complaint
- outcomes
  —by category
  —by specific change/action

This is a set of elements thought necessary both for information
system effectiveness and for demonstrating ombudsman impact to
the clients of the system (Ziegenfuss, Charette, and Guenin, 1984).

The above elements mean that a user receives a categorization
of complaints by frequency, some sense of the nature of the
complaints, an indication of who the complaining employees or
customers are (by group type), and importantly, a summary of what
has been done by the organization in response. The data is
communicated in writing via reports and orally by the troubleshooter, the latter method usually being most effective in terms of
understanding and acceptance.

Step 7: Specify Procedures and Operational Conditions   In
the final step, all procedures and operational conditions are
specified, from who will be on the list to receive the reports to exact
days of delivery and who will do the typing. Nearly all organizations have experience with data report preparation and distribution,
so there is little need to elaborate on the basics.

There are two major concerns about the information system
that almost always emerge through the design process (and they
should). First, there is much concern about the confidentiality of the

data. How can this information flow through the organization without the complainant/clients being concerned that their confidences are violated? Second, there is concern that the development and distribution of the information would take so much of the troubleshooter's time that he or she becomes essentially a bureaucrat, as opposed to a people-oriented problem solver.

The first issue—confidentiality—can be solved by agreement that all data presentations are in aggregate; no individual complaints are described. This means that at the start it is not possible to provide complaint data in detail to a single department. Without multiple complaints, the subjects would be too easily identified. Whether to identify the location of the complaint is one of the more difficult problems. Some discretion is required until sufficient complaints in each unit are filed to fully mask identity. Even then, when in doubt, case-specific data should not be reported.

The issue of work time consumption by the data system is solved by keeping the reports simple and standardized. One-page reports with no tailoring for individuals is the rule. These are feasible without the time burdens required for development, analysis, and distribution of unique information. Individual analysis can be done for departments on a request basis.

We must now consider what troubleshooters and the organization get out of the data system.

Benefits and Outcomes of Information Circulation

During the troubleshooter program start-up, there is a special need to identify what the founders perceive to be the data system outcomes, the expected benefits of communicating this information. Troubleshooter communication based on complaint data and experience

- helps to reinforce organizational goals and values and culture building
- fosters dialogue about problems
- provides data for technical and structural problem detection
- contributes to human relations problem identification

- is part of the data base for management development, review, and control

These contributions from the troubleshooter as communicator represent some of the impact of the troubleshooter program (further discussed in Chapter Ten). Because data system and communication payoffs are critical, they will be discussed briefly.

The first communication benefit is reinforcement of goals and values, a part of the culture building and culture maintenance activity that all organizations must have. The information on complaints and responses helps indicate whether the culture that the chief executive, senior executives, board, and employees want to build and maintain is supported by responses to problems. For example, many public and private executives insist that open communication and confrontation of problems is a core value of their corporation or public agency. Information about how their organization responds to the troubleshooter's complaints informs these executives of whether there is support for or undercutting of that value. If used responsibly, actions taken to address the complaints reinforce the core values, helping the organization achieve its goal of open communication. Writ large, this kind of goal/value maintenance ensures that the corporate culture continues to develop as desired by the senior management group.

An example here is the firing of Ralph Hansen for policy violation. This is a message to employees about the nature of the corporate culture. There are severe penalties for rule violation, and importantly, these penalties may be invoked in what might be thought of as a transitional period. To the employee, this message means "beware." Is this the message executives want to send to employees?

Second, the communication helps to foster open discussion of problems. Problem confrontation and dialogue is difficult for all organizations, often requiring a facilitator, a role the troubleshooter plays. Using the data to open a dialogue, the troubleshooter helps managers and employees to think through the problem and create change actions.

Technical and structural troubleshooting is done as a result of the complaint reviews. Employees do not want to confront and address technical and structural problems, particularly when professional opinions differ. Information formally notifying the corporation that these problems exist, for example, in production, sabotage, professionalism, and quality control helps to ensure that the organization cannot duck its corrective responsibilities. The fact that information on problems exists and is circulating increases the probability that someone in the organization will move to correct them. Managers and employees are less able to avoid addressing what other organizational members know are problems (they are out in the open).

Troubleshooter communication also becomes part of a human relations monitoring system. The data helps to identify problems in morale, conflict, expectations, and insecurity that arise in all organizations, especially when major changes in structure or function are occurring. Additionally, the problem data helps in guiding and reorienting the human relations executives by providing them with information on the current system and with ideas about what must be done.

Furthermore, troubleshooter communication actively supports a range of management activities through five key areas: planning, organizing, developing, directing/leading, and controlling. Each of these is aided by information from complaints. Complaint data can be used for identifying organizational change needs for planning action. Data is used to develop managers by testing their leadership abilities in correcting problems. Last, complaints are a performance control indicator—high numbers of complaints in one unit mean problems. This can be seen as negative, as something to hide, or it can be seen as providing the data to establish a plan for correction and continued organizational development.

Summary

This chapter reviewed the troubleshooter's involvement in information gathering and distribution—the communications aspects of the troubleshooter program. Topics included communication purposes, the information system design and operations, and seven steps used to create a data system to support troubleshooter communication work. Finally, the benefits of communication were outlined. The data from the complaints can be used for organizational development, for identifying barriers to productivity, and for creating a culture that relies on open communication and problem solving.

7

A Day in the Life
of an Organizational Troubleshooter

Introduction

One of the best ways to understand what a troubleshooter does is to sample a "typical" day. This chapter outlines a troubleshooter's activities from one day's start to close. It is a representative day, although this particular set of activities is a composite of a number of days of activities. Activities are obviously not the same every day and it is unlikely that any one troubleshooter would have a day exactly like this. The variation in the tasks and nature of the work activities during the day is much like general troubleshooter work, though. It does represent the work of troubleshooter colleagues who have read this description of a sample day.

As you will see in the following pages, a day in a troubleshooter's life can involve a wide-ranging set of activities, including

- interviewing complaint presenters
- taking phone calls
- investigating old complaints by checking files
- meeting with attorneys to resolve complaints that have already gone too far
- active listening and personal counseling
- writing the report
- meeting with complainants to counsel them about seeking assistance elsewhere
- making referrals to various other offices within the corporation

113

At the conclusion of the review, the outstanding characteristics of a typical day in the life of the troubleshooter are summarized. The description is presented as if one troubleshooter were telling the story of his or her daily activities.

This troubleshooter is a formally recognized ombudsman in a corporation of 3,200 employees. The report is in the first person, written as if the ombudsman offered this in a conversational account of a day's work. It is a daily diary.

An Ombudsman's Day

8:30 A.M. I frequently begin my day by completing complaint reports from the previous day. I have to admit that as a people-oriented person, the notion that I have to write reports is somewhat objectionable. I am much more interested in the meetings with complainants and in the group sessions with department heads, managers, and employees that I use to resolve the problems.

I can usually get some of the reports written first thing before I lose my ability to control my time. I begin by spending about half an hour writing up complaint reports. The reports include the facts collected as a part of investigation, summary thoughts on ways the complaint could be resolved, people with whom I have already talked and those with whom I have yet to talk, and some target times I expect can be met for successful resolution of the complaint.

I tend to rough these reports out quickly, passing them on to my secretary. I have found that once the reports have been at least partially committed to paper, it is easier for me to edit them, refining as I go along.

9:00 A.M. If I have no early morning complaint appointments or meeting sessions, I am usually doing some background investigative work. This morning I need to check files relating to old policy statements on sex discrimination within the organization. I recently had a complaint from a female employee who was beginning to feel that she was a victim of discrimination. She was not aware of any policies against sex discrimination that the organization had developed during her ten years of employment and thought that it had not done very much to combat the problem. She wanted to know if the lack of policy was one of the key points to her case, or at least an indicator of the depth of the problem.

Inquiring at the personnel office, I found that there was a history of policy proclamations on this issue dating back to 1978. I quickly noted the number of policy statements and their starting dates so I could pass this information back to the complainant. Then I asked personnel to send me copies of the policy statements so that I could see how their content would affect this case.

9:15 A.M. Before I could follow up a bit more with the woman who filed the sex discrimination question, the phone rang. My caller wanted to file a complaint about management relations and concerns about certain production areas. Like most of my callers, he wasn't sure how to file a complaint. Although the company had announced the opening of my office and clearly displayed my phone number on bulletin boards and in the company directory, nearly every caller was not sure I was the person to contact. And despite my "publicity," nearly everyone who called heard about me from a friend of a friend of a friend that I had helped. I mentioned that I was open to taking a wide range of complaints, but if he was a union member and wanted to file a formal grievance, that was his first option. I asked him to use his union first. He stated that he was not in the union and that his complaint had to do with some questions about quality control in production.

The caller provided some of the details of the question, and it sounded significant enough for us to meet in person. He said he would try to bring along some further information outlining his case. We made an appointment to meet in two days.

9:30 A.M.—Interview At 9:30 A.M., I had my first complaint interview of the morning. An engineer came in from one of the divisions with a complaint about the manager of his unit. The manager was an engineer in his late thirties. The complaining engineer was fifty-nine years old, just about to turn sixty. The manager had talked to him about trying to increase the speed of his work. After several discussions in which the pace of the work was a concern, the manager suggested that perhaps he was slowing down and nearing retirement.

The complainant felt that this was "not so subtle" pressure to retire! He wanted to know whether or not this was age discrimination. But more important, the engineer was concerned about retaining his job and rebuilding a working relationship. He frankly noted that he didn't have much of an understanding on how to speed up his work and would like some further information in that area. We talked for about half an hour. I suggested that we meet again in two days after I had an opportunity to talk to the manager and to see what kind of assistance I could get for him.

10:00 A.M.—Meeting with Lawyers I next attended a meeting with two of the corporate attorneys. They had been told that one former employee had sued us over concerns with his dismissal. The employee was angry about the dismissal, thinking it was unfair and that he had not had an opportunity to address the concerns for which he had been dismissed. His brief, filed by his lawyers, insisted that the organization had no mechanism for filing complaints in-house and, secondarily, did not encourage employees and managers to resolve their problems.

The attorneys wanted to know how widespread the knowledge of my existence was in the organization and whether or not this particular employee had used the system. This raised two rather delicate questions. First, we needed to consider how widespread the existence of my program was within the organization—a subtle review of both the extent of my recognition and my power. The second issue was potentially much more significant. The question was, had this former employee ever used my services as a complaint resolution expert within the organization? We stress that complaint information is confidential. The concern was that if I informed them that the employee used the ombudsman, it would be a violation of confidentiality. The problem was rather easily resolved in this case, since I was able to answer freely that he had never used the system.

After some further discussion about the nature of the case, the lawyers said that there was a chance it would be negotiated out of court. They asked whether or not I would consider being involved in the mediation of the dispute. I remarked that I would be glad to do anything they thought would be helpful, but only as a neutral party.

10:45 A.M.—A No-Follow-Up Problem with an Old Complaint   Since I was in the attorney's office, I realized I was not far from one of the managers' offices who was involved in a prior complaint. I thought I would drop in to see how the proposed actions to resolve the problem were working. I already knew that, to date, no action had been taken. The complainant had called me with regard to the continuing problem of smoking in an office suite. The complainant could not tolerate the smoking and suggested that it be controlled or that he be moved to a no-smoking suite. The manager felt that person should continue to be part of his team and so far had taken no action.

I wanted to encourage the manager to try to take care of the situation before it got worse, but he was not in. Just as I was about to leave, he did come in, but by then I had to rush to an 11:00 A.M. meeting. He quickly told me he had not taken action yet but seemed willing to get cracking on the problem. I made a mental note to get back to him the very next morning.

11:00 A.M.—Counseling   At 11:00 A.M., I had a meeting with a junior manager from one of the marketing divisions. This manager was concerned about her performance to date and particularly how it would affect her promotional possibilities. She had an M.B.A. from a reputable school and was concerned that she was not moving up quickly enough in the corporate hierarchy. She seemed to have some definite notions about how quickly she should be at what level in the organization. She was concerned that her performance was not measuring up. In a previous session, she stated that some of her performance problems were related to unfair treatment by senior managers in her unit. She felt they were threatened by her youth and her energy and enthusiasm.

She had been with the company about one and a half years. It seemed to me that in this second session, I was really engaged in counseling the young woman. The problem was at least in part her own insecurities and anxieties stemming from her youth, the fact that she was new in the corporation, and the fact that this was her first job following graduate school.

This second session was useful, I thought, even though a preliminary probing of that unit did not turn up any harassment by senior managers. This counseling provided needed reassurance for the young woman and would probably help to avoid problems with senior management. If she continued to have this type of problem, I would suggest a referral to a professional counselor, either inside the corporation or outside it.

11:25 A.M.—Report Writing   At this point, with a few spare minutes before lunch, I went back to writing complaint reports from the previous day. This allowed me to get some of this out of the way before lunch, clearing my desk for the afternoon sessions. The afternoon sessions rarely ended early, so this was all the report writing for today.

12:00 Noon—Lunch with the EEO Representative   I scheduled a lunch with the Equal Employment Opportunity representative in our corporation, Jane Thomas. We met at a small restaurant across the street, since whenever we meet in the employees' cafeteria there is talk by management that we are conspiring to make their jobs more difficult. This is a regular monthly meeting that we use to ensure that we are working well on cross-referrals. We also use it to clear up any questions that we might have in our own complaint taking that closely involved each other's area. This is the technical side.

Since we are both basically in the same work, the meeting is also a support session. Obviously, the EEO representative understands the stresses and trials and tribulations of the corporate ombudsman's work and vice versa. It's an opportunity for us to commiserate about the difficulties in promoting change with people and in confronting and resolving the problems in the corporation at large. I finish the lunch refreshed.

1:05 P.M.—Call from Colleague   After lunch, I return a call from a colleague concerning promotion for this year's corporate ombudsman conference. The Corporate Ombudsman Association, of which I am a member, is trying to develop a network among ombudsmen in major private corporations across the country. There are several reasons for this linkage. One key reason is the support and assistance each ombudsman will receive in developing his or her own job and role in their corporation. The association also promotes the existence of the ombudsmen around the country, furthering the concept of in-house problem solving. It parallels other ombudsman groups such as the Patient Representative Society of the American Hospital Association. And last, it gives companies an opportunity to publicly link with other corporations that are already engaged in this activity. We spend about twenty minutes talking about mailing lists and persons to contact.

1:30 P.M.—Chief Executive Officer Briefing At 1:30 P.M., I meet with the chief executive officer to brief him on the status of the complaints I was taking in the corporation. The CEO was particularly interested in hearing the employee's perspective on how we were doing. This emerges from the nature of the complaints and exactly what the corporation was doing to resolve them. His concerns were (1) that the corporation was seen as responsive, (2) that he was informed about what employees felt about the corporation and how things were going, and (3) how the corporation was doing in resolving complaints (to keep down the cost of litigation and low productivity). The company had just lost a multimillion dollar suit by a former employee. The CEO knew that the court award was only a part of the cost of resolving the problem. There were a lot of hidden staff expenses in preparing for the litigation, as well as attorneys' fees and finally the settlement. He had *no interest* in his management or his employees generating follow-up cases.

I followed a general pattern for the monthly briefing that we had established at the outset. I gave him a simple one-page summary of the volume of complaints from the different divisions, the nature of the complaints in each of the divisions, and a short list of examples of the problems—a phrase or a sentence, explanations of the nature of the complaint. This type of report gave him a sense of "the numbers" in terms of how they were doing, and also a more extensive understanding of the nature of the problems, without overburdening him with details.

We talked briefly about the strategies that I am using to resolve the complaints. He offered to be of any further assistance I might need in carrying on with the job, specifically suggesting that I could feel free to call on the corporation's attorneys for help.

2:15 P.M.—In-Person Complaint   Following the CEO briefing, I returned to my office to take another complaint.

This complaint involved research work in one of the laboratories. The complainant was a young and dedicated scientist in the industrial research and development laboratory. She was working as a part of a new-product team that was developing a new artificial sweetener. One afternoon, she noticed a discrepancy in one senior scientist's reports and checked it. It appeared he was "fudging" the data but she was not sure. He was an irascible guy. Since he would be responsible for her promotions and her continued work on the project, she was afraid to ask him about it. She did not want to embarrass or anger him and had no idea what to do, so she just watched and worried, becoming more and more distracted.

This was the first time I heard this complaint. I listened attentively, asking her for details about what data, when was it altered, how much, by whom, did she have proof or was it speculation.

I told her that I would begin to look into the case but would not yet confront the other scientist nor would I reveal that she was the complainant. She left feeling satisfied that a start was made.

I thought that I should begin by asking general questions about the type of problem to several senior scientists who I knew well. I also needed time to think through a verification strategy (that I thought would be most challenging). I made a note to move quickly on it.

3:00 P.M.—Referral to the Employee Assistance Program   At 3:00 P.M., I took a call from an employee who was concerned about his colleague's drinking on the job. He wanted to complain in some ways but also wanted to ensure that his colleague would receive some assistance. He was asking if I could help with this problem and/or what he should do as a start. We talked about the nature of the difficulty and the level of the problem; was it a beginning problem, a fairly well-developed one, or at an absolute crisis stage with danger involved? If it were the latter, I would join him immediately on the unit and see if we couldn't get some action today. He remarked, however, that he felt it was more in the developing stage but that it was clearly a pattern and one that was getting progressively worse.

I suggested that the best referral was to the employee assistance program, which specifically dealt with personal problems of employees on the job. I gave him the name and telephone number of the director of that unit, suggesting that he start there. I told him to get back to me within a day to inform me of progress. If he needed additional assistance, I would make sure that he received it.

3:30 P.M.—Referee for Two-Manager Conflict   At 3:30 P.M., I worked on the resolution to a problem that involved two managers with joint control over an employee in both of their units. This company is operated with a matrix organizational design that combines functional areas with specific project teams. The problem involved an organizational development specialist who reported to the human resources vice president and who was working on a project team to develop a new product for the company. The product team leader requested that the organization development specialist assist him in some team relations work that the organization development specialist felt would not be productive. The team leader wanted to mandate a two-day weekend sensitivity group to "shape up" employee attitudes. When this problem was raised with the two managers, they immediately got into a shouting match because of past conflicts and communication problems. They were not able to resolve it. The organization development specialist suggested that I sit in to try to referee the meeting.

The meeting was heavily emotional and very tense, not what you would call the lighter part of my day. However, we were able to discuss it with a somewhat lowered or at least controlled level of emotional involvement. We were able to arrive at a temporary compromise by which the request would be put on hold until we found a successful way around the methodological barrier and the conflict in objectives.

5:00 P.M.—Conclusions At the end of the day, I had a bit of time before I would leave. I spent this time completing reports, returning phone calls from employees who wanted to file complaints, and setting up a management team briefing, which I also give each month.

7:00 P.M.—Follow-Up I thought I was done for today, but I had a telephone call from a senior computer scientist. He was angry about a management decision to cut back financial support for his project. He told me about it the other day, feeling that the decision was a result of internal politics. He was talking now about his severe disappointment and that he may want to get even. I agreed to meet him for coffee. When we met, he was very upset, implying that both suicide and sabotage were options for him. We talked for two hours, after which he agreed to sleep on it until we met again the next day.

I went home to bed emotionally and physically exhausted.

Summary

The diary just presented reflected a day in the life of a formal corporate ombudsman. Consumer ombudsmen such as patient representatives and "unrecognized ombudsmen" such as executive assistants, employee and human relations managers, and others tend to have the same kind of day. They take complaints, make written and oral reports, meet with their referral and support networks, and counsel members of the organization. Except for labels and the types of persons seen, a day in the life of a corporate troubleshooter is a somewhat standard one—it can be generalized to many/most troubleshooters.

What does this summary of one day of troubleshooting activity tell us about the characteristics of the job? The following general job traits emerge:

- *Varied*

  As one can see from the above set of activities, the day is full of very different tasks—it's a nonroutine job.

- *Interesting*

  All of the aspects of the job are interesting. The complaints are not boring; they're unique and individual problems.

- *People-oriented*

  This is a "people" job from start to finish, involving talking, interacting, resolving, mediating.

- *Hectic*

  This is a fairly typical day, in which there are many activities scheduled back to back. The activities are often very different, and so the pace is more hectic and harried than serene.

- *Unpredictable*

  While the days themselves are somewhat predictable, the nature of the problems and the tasks on any given day are fairly unpredictable.

- *Stressful*

  Any time you are dealing with people and their conflicts, stress is high. Mediating these conflicts is a high-stress job.

- *Lacking in closure*

  Most of the tasks initiated on any given day are never actually finished on that day; thus you don't often get the sense of final closure to a problem.

- *Rewarding*

  There is keen awareness that you're removing barriers to productivity and increasing the quality of working life of fellow employees in the corporation.

- *Technically challenging*

  The work requires a very high level of interpersonal competence and clinical/counseling/negotiation/teaching skills.

In short, this is a day that is interesting, that requires no clock-watching, and that is highly demanding and fulfilling on a level much like a combination of clinical work and highly successful management productivity. The cases presented in Chapter Eight will further demonstrate these characteristics.

8

Troubleshooting Experiences:
Learning That All Problems
Are Important

Introduction

One way to further understand the nature of the troubleshooter's job is to examine a set of cases. Of course, an individual trouble-shooter may have more of one type of case than another, and not all of the topics treated here will be addressed by a troubleshooter during a given period of time. This casebook chapter concentrates on cases presented by employees on the following complaint topics: research data fudging, interdepartmental conflict, discrimination, supervisory conflict, sexual harassment, physical conditions, salary, personal problems, and production/sabotage. Some of these cases will appear to be more important than others (for example, sexual harassment and sabotage versus hot work areas); however, it should be remembered that a troubleshooter considers *all* problems important, since some less significant ones eventually point to larger conflicts.

In each of the cases, an abstract of the troubleshooter's actions is presented that touches on the five common steps of identification, investigation, feedback of facts, development of responses, and monitoring to ensure follow-up action. In all of the cases, the responses are sketched in extremely brief fashion. They are offered to provide a flavor of casework, not exhaustive detail. Also, it is important to keep in mind that many readers will perceive the problems and the responses as having alternative interpretations, with many options for other action. That is true of nearly all cases, and attests to the difficulty of the work.

Case 1: Research Data Fudging

The Complaint Tom Rodriguez was a five-year employee working as a marketing researcher in a food-products company. He had been involved in studies of various products and their market research potential since his arrival at the company. He was mostly a "numbers cruncher" without very much exposure to the committee meetings and board briefings at which his numbers were presented. His supervisors were increasingly interested in moving him up the market research ladder in the corporation, especially in the last year.

At the conclusion of a recent study, he was asked by the market research director (to whom he reports) to make a presentation to the new-product group of the corporation. The market research director said a quick review of the data from the new study would be useful, suggesting that he and Tom should go over it prior to the briefing.

During the briefing about two days later, the director saw that the market data did not reflect strong support for the new product. Noting this, he suggested that some changes could be made. Tom was not clear about this and asked specifically what he was talking about. The director suggested that new products were tough to get off the ground in this corporation. The way it was usually done, he said, was that the market studies were conducted but the data was "boosted" by a factor of about 20 percent. He suggested applying this factor to the data to show greater market support.

He said that the senior officers in the corporation were generally too conservative to adopt new product ideas very easily, but if they saw strong market data support, they generally went ahead. Almost always, these product ideas were successful. He couched it in an "overcoming the bureaucracy" sort of concept and strongly suggested that Tom do it.

Since this suggestion was followed by a comment on the possibility of Tom's moving up the career ladder, he went to the troubleshooter for consultation on what he should do about it.

Troubleshooter Actions   The complaint as the trouble-shooter saw it was a dual one involving both the ethics of the decision to "fudge the data" and the issue of corporate culture. The troubleshooter investigated, asking some of his contacts whether this was, in fact, true. The investigation uncovered that it was generally the case. Data fudging was a bit of a time-honored tradition for breaking through the corporate conservatism.

The troubleshooter asked the market research director about the situation, which he at first denied. When the troubleshooter mentioned that he had confirmation from other independent sources, the director admitted it was true. He had no suggestions on what to do about it. He could choose to play it straight but he did not feel it would be helpful to the company. He also did not want the issue to focus on him personally, saying he was only one of six market research directors.

The troubleshooter suggested that it could be taken to the executive group as a problem using a product or products that were established some five years ago. The market research director agreed that that might open the topic, which then could be expanded to address corporate conservatism. The troubleshooter agreed to do that as a first response and reported this back to the complainant.

The troubleshooter saw this as both an individual-level problem (one employee/one conflict) and a system-level problem (corporate culture and values issue).

Case 2: Interdepartmental Conflict

The Complaint   The troubleshooter received a complaint from Harold Thompson in the computer product services depart-ment. Harold was concerned that customer demands on product services were becoming too heavy. Customers were becoming dissatisfied about the timeliness with which the corporation could respond and whether or not the company was being forthright in terms of how quickly responses were made. He complained that the salesmen were saying that product services were available practi-cally twenty-four hours a day. When customers called, they *expected* immediate attention. When they had to wait several days for a response, it was quite disconcerting, to say the least.

Both the sales department and the product services director were aware of the problem. However, the two directors did not get along and were not able to even hold a discussion regarding the problem. This was attempted some four or five months ago, but the meeting quickly dissolved into a shouting match and was ended before any useful suggestions emerged. Harold only knew that at his level, customers were unhappy. Even when he was able to address the customers' problems, they were dissatisfied because of the time delay (mostly an expectations problem, he felt). Harold could see that increasing dissatisfaction among customers would result in a detrimental effect on the company at some point in the future.

He asked for suggestions on how to handle the interdepartmental conflict.

Troubleshooter Actions   The troubleshooter agreed to look into the case, suggesting he would be talking with other employees in both units before he talked to the respective department directors. This he did, finding that the complaint was essentially true. The obvious first action seemed to be to initiate a meeting of the two department directors with the troubleshooter as third-party mediator.

The meeting was held. Both directors at first expressed surprise over the existence of the problem. On assurance that it was fairly evident from the employees, they both admitted its existence. A one-hour session probing possible solutions degenerated into a near shouting match. The troubleshooter suggested another meeting to try to resolve it independently, without higher involvement. The directors agreed, but that meeting too was unsuccessful. Some possibilities for department changes emerged, but they could not be agreed on.

The troubleshooter requested a third meeting, to which he invited their already informed senior vice president (after telling them he would do this). Both were emotional and somewhat stubborn but were able to resolve it with the senior VP present at the next meeting.

The troubleshooter would continue to follow up on the meeting's action plans over the next six months.

Case 3: Discrimination

The Complaint Mary Matthews filed a complaint about discrimination in her office. She was a junior marketing representative who was interested in promotion to marketing services coordinator. The district supervisor had been very nice to her on hiring and remarked at the time that it was "quite nice to have a woman and a black, no less, in the business." Mary had long grown accustomed to snide comments about her gender and her race and just sloughed it off.

However, three sales representative coordinator positions had come open in the last two years. She was eligible and applied for each one. However, she did not get any of the jobs. After the third final selection was made, she went to the district manager and asked directly what the problem was.

Although he made no direct references, he did suggest that it was important to have a good match between the personnel coordinating the team and the makeup of the team. He did not offer to explain this and Mary did not follow up with additional questions.

She remarked to the troubleshooter that, in part, she was afraid that she already knew the answer. She was unsure how the company felt with regard to racial and sex discrimination and wanted first to know what official positions were, as well as what informal actions have been taken in the past. She also wanted advice on how to handle the problem.

At the same time, she remarked that her father was an attorney active with the NAACP. If she did not get satisfaction within the company, she intended to take it further and expected to receive full support at home.

Troubleshooter Actions The troubleshooter investigated the complaint, finding that Mary Matthews' allegations were true. Three positions were open; she had applied for all three. In the last two cases, it appeared that she was more qualified than the persons selected. The troubleshooter asked the district supervisor about his selection process. He informed the troubleshooter that it was his decision (with clear resentment at the probing).

The troubleshooter thought this case had potentially significant impact on the corporation both as a guide/model and in terms of potential litigation cost. The troubleshooter went to the senior vice president for personnel, who immediately initated his own review. He called in the district supervisor, who admitted that the case was valid. The supervisor was given a one-week suspension without pay. He was directed to redesign the marketing services system to make room for one more coordinator, based on an expected expansion that was emerging. This was not satisfactory to the district supervisor, but it was accepted.

The complainant was satisfied with the corporation's response and her own new situation as the fourth sales representative coordinator.

The troubleshooter suggested that the corporation present a training program on recruitment and promotion policies and practices. This was done, but only on a one-time basis in two of the departments.

Case 4: Supervisory Conflict

The Complaint   Frank Smith filed a complaint regarding what he felt to be unfair treatment from his supervisor, foreman John Thompson. Frank was a single parent whose wife had passed away a year ago. He had two small children, ages six and eight. Frank's job began officially at 8:30. However, he informed the foreman that in order to get the children safely off to school, it was difficult for him to leave the house before 8:30. He asked if he could make up the fifteen minutes either over lunch or at the close of the day, when a neighbor was already watching the children.

He noted that his job on the shop floor was independent. He could start fifteen minutes later than his colleagues without impeding work in any way. Since his colleagues were also aware of the situation with the small children, he did not feel that they would object to this special treatment. He communicated his request to the foreman.

He reported that the foreman expressed shock at the request and insisted that absolutely not, under any circumstances, could this be done. After several days, he went to the foreman and made the request again, suggesting that there was no easy way for him to arrange babysitting for a fifteen-minute period the first thing in the morning. The foreman insisted that there was no way he could start a new company precedent allowing individuals to receive special treatment. Frank did not want to make trouble, but at the same time, he did not know how he could continue his job and care for his children. He asked if there was any way that he could get help with this problem.

Troubleshooter Actions   The troubleshooter "investigation" was brief. He needed to establish the school and work times and the character of Frank Smith's job. This he could do with some telephone calls. The troubleshooter then went to the shop floor manager to see what might be done in the way of a response. He suggested that he would be afraid that many persons would want this kind of exception.

The troubleshooter then went to the personnel executive to see if "flextime" was being considered or had ever been discussed. He said it had not but that he had read much about it and would be interested. The troubleshooter suggested using this one employee's problem as part of a pilot test. The personnel executive agreed.

The troubleshooter organized a meeting with the personnel executive and the shop floor manager to talk it over. The group agreed that it seemed an ideal case. The group then brought in the foreman and discussed the problem and this proposed solution. He was reluctant at first but gradually became convinced of the fairness (or at least recognized the pressure). He was somewhat interested in the possibilities, mostly negative.

This new arrangement was done. The troubleshooter monitored it after three months to see if it was working well, which it was.

Case 5: Sexual Harassment

The Complaint   The troubleshooter received a telephone call one day from Kathleen Collins, a computer systems marketing representative in the local division of the company. Kathleen had not been with the company more than about nine months but was now having a problem with the district manager for computer systems marketing. He travels with her on her marketing trips about once per month to supervise and to offer suggestions for performance improvement. The first three trips were very professional. But on the last several trips he made suggestions about their need to travel overnight and about the possibility of sharing accommodations.

The suggestions for "accommodations sharing" were at first very subtle and were offered in somewhat of a joking fashion. As the suggestions continued, she said she expressed no interest at all. His suggestions then became more direct and during the last trip, somewhat strident.

Kathleen said that she was concerned that her performance ratings would suffer and that her career with the company could be in jeopardy. She had had no performance ratings since the start of the suggestions, but was due for one in three months.

She had never encountered this in her quite young career and did not know how to handle it. She was asking for guidance on how to discourage the advances in a way that would protect her job and career. Also, since she liked her supervisor, she did not want to offend him.

Troubleshooter Actions   In this case, it was not necessary to further identify the nature of the complaint. Typically, an investigation would involve the confrontation of the supervisor with the question of "did this happen?" The troubleshooter asked Kathleen if she would like to try once more to discourage him (with some guidance) or would she like the troubleshooter to confront the man with the question directly? Or a simple "general visit" to marketing to raise the question could be made.

She said that there was another trip well before her ratings were due. She would be willing to try once more to stop the advances. After that, she definitely wanted outside help. She also wanted a record that she complained, since she was afraid of the impact on her ratings.

The troubleshooter agreed to this as well, informing her that frequently "merely inquiring" into the problem was sufficient intervention. The troubleshooter also suggested that he could send a policy memorandum/reminder to the marketing department. Sometimes this was effective.

The troubleshooter and Kathleen decided that another try from her, the policy reminder, and the troubleshooter's beginning inquiry would be the response. They agreed to meet after her next trip.

Case 6: Physical Conditions

The Complaint Martha Worthington filed a complaint about conditions in one of the manufacturing sections that developed components for computers. She noted that she was in one of the old buildings in one of the old wings that was scheduled to be renovated in the next few years. She noted that in the summer, temperatures in the building climbed into the mid to high nineties on hot days.

When she and the other workers complained about the conditions, they were informed that the company would not invest in air-conditioning for this old building. They were told that it was about to be renovated. However, they were first told this about a year and a half ago but no work had begun. When she raised the question again, she was told to drop it.

She said she simply wanted to get across the point that their productivity was suffering, since by early afternoon most of the workers were going at about half-speed or less because of the heat. She thought that an investment in some sort of portable air-conditioners would probably be recouped by the additional productivity. She wanted to know how to express these concerns without getting herself fired.

Troubleshooter Actions The troubleshooter investigated the situation by talking to several other employees of that unit. They confirmed the problem, which the troubleshooter further verified by walking into the unit one afternoon. It was unbearable.

The troubleshooter then contacted building maintenance to see what could be done. They said they were already backed up with projects and were constrained by a limited budget. The troubleshooter suggested the productivity problem might be costing more, but that assessment was clearly beyond their level of concern.

The troubleshooter then went to the operations vice president, who did recognize the problem (and did recognize the troubleshooter's power to force resolution if necessary). He thought there might be an intervening step that could be taken. Perhaps portable air-conditioners and fans could be leased for the summer. He would request a quick engineering and cost review.

This was investigated and found to be feasible without too high a cost. It was completed ten days later.

Case 7: Salary

The Complaint Barbara Bosworth filed a complaint regarding her secretarial salary. She had been with the corporation for some five years, beginning as a Secretary I. She had recently advanced to Secretary III and was making $19,500 a year. She was interested in further promotion but knew that the next rung on the career ladder for her was administrative assistant. When she had an opportunity to be transferred to another unit, she jumped at it, thinking that this was the chance to become an administrative assistant. When the job was offered to her, she neglected to ask to be sure that the official title said administrative assistant. The administrator interviewing her referred to the jobholder as his assistant, who would be pretty much in control of the office. When the decision was made, he informed her that she would get a 5 percent jump immediately and another 5 percent in three months after satisfactory performance.

After three months, she realized that she was working as an administrative assistant pretty much in control of the office as he had suggested. However, she did not hear mention of any forthcoming 5 percent salary increase. When she raised the issue, he said he felt her salary was appropriate for her duties. She remarked that her responsibilities were considerably beyond what she was doing as Secretary III and that the new higher salary after three months' satisfactory performance was one of the conditions of the job. He did not respond but looked fairly agitated about her suggesting the point.

She did not know how to pursue this issue further, but felt that she was unfairly treated with regard to salary and the movement to the new position. She was afraid that pushing it further with her boss would cause her problems on the job and wanted to know how to handle the situation. She remarked that she would not stay in the job without additional salary.

Troubleshooter Actions   The troubleshooter investigated the situation by examining her work load and duties and comparative salaries. She was correct in her assessment. The troubleshooter passed this information on to the personnel director, who reviewed the case and agreed. The personnel director called in her supervisor (a private meeting) and suggested that he revise her salary to fit her new duties and responsibilities. The man was immediately compliant with the request, seeming to be afraid of consequences if he did not. He offered only a halfhearted presentation of his position.

Case 8: Personal Problems—Addictions and Marriage

The Complaint   David Stern was a relatively young sales representative in a district manager's office. He was one of a crack team put together by an equally young district manager who was beating the competition easily. David was a friend of the district manager, since they had gone to school together. He was aware that the pace of sales was quick and that it was important for the district manager to take clients out to lunch quite frequently. However, David noted that his young boss seemed to be indulging in more lunchtime martinis than he had seen him drink in the early part of their careers. He also knew, since their wives were friends, that his district manager and his wife were having marital problems.

He felt that these two difficulties—the heavier drinking, which he was not sure was really an addiction, and the marriage problems—were linked. He wanted to suggest to his friend that he seek treatment or seek some sort of support but did not know how to go about it or even whether the suggestion was appropriate in the work context. He also knew that the district manager was becoming increasingly short-tempered with the staff. They had had very good working relationships over the past five years.

He wanted to know two things: whether it was appropriate to raise the addiction and marital issue in the work context at all (or whether he should just raise it as a friend out of work at some point), and whether or not the organization had assistance available for this kind of problem.

Troubleshooter Actions   The troubleshooter spent some time telling David about the policies of the corporation and the programs the corporation has for addressing the personal problems of employees. The company had long supported assistance as a means of retaining good people.

The troubleshooter referred him to the employee assistance program director, who would offer a series of strategies for getting help to his friend. This was to be done quickly. The troubleshooter called while David was there to set up the appointment. The troubleshooter talked a bit more about the usual forms of help—the educational role—and suggested that he call back in a month to report on progress.

Case 9: Production/Sabotage

The Complaint   Ronald Smith filed a complaint relating to difficulties on the computer assembly line. Someone in the line appeared to be sabotaging some of the equipment during the production process. He was aware that some of his supervisors understood that there was a problem, but no one seemed to know quite how to deal with it. He had been approached on one or two occasions to ask if it was his doing. He did not admit to it being his problem, nor did he know who was responsible on the line. Although the supervisors leaned on him heavily, they did not discover the cause of the problem.

All he knew was that the defects showing up in the assembly line seemed to be a regular and purposeful process. It was not the kind of mistake that would be made easily without some conscious attempt to do so.

Troubleshooter Actions The troubleshooter's brief investigation suggested that this seemed to be a real sabotage problem. The products were at the technological cutting edge and were of special concern to the company. The troubleshooter immediately referred the problem to plant security after telling the complainant what he would do. The complainant agreed to help security with the problem, which was regarded as significant, possibly criminal, and well beyond the people-conflict situation.

Customer Complaints

To represent troubleshooters that handle customer problems, the casebook must also include illustrative customer complaints. These complaints are similar to ones mentioned throughout the book, and are handled in essentially the same manner as those of employees. The following cases indicate examples of customer problems handled by troubleshooters. The complaints involve or come from a patient, a prisoner, a citizen, a welfare recipient, and a customer of a gas company.

Case 10: The Patient's Treatment

The Complaint Two parents were at a dinner party one evening when the host received a telephone call. The caller asked to speak to one of them. The caller informed Mr. Jones that his three-year-old son was in the hospital and that he needed permission to treat him. The father, obviously upset, said, "What hospital? What's going on?" His grandparents were babysitting with him. The caller identified himself as a physician and asked for permission to treat. Mr. Jones said, "Well, I need more information," whereupon the physician said, "I need permission to treat your son. Will you give it?" Mr. Jones replied that he would not give permission until he knew about the nature of the problem and what was going on, whereupon the physician hung up.

The next person to call was the nurse, who called back within a couple of minutes and said, "Your son has fallen and cut his head. We need permission to treat." This time Mrs. Jones answered, and asked for further information. The nurse said, "It's a fairly deep gash in his forehead requiring probably seven to fifteen stitches. Do we have permission?" Mrs. Jones said, "Is he basically okay?" The nurse said, "Yes, but we need permission to clean and close the wound." Mrs. Jones said, "That's fine with me; my parents will monitor. Go ahead." She hung up. The next call was from her mother, the boy's grandmother. She said, "They need permission to do this, but will not accept our permission." Mrs. Jones said, "Okay. Tell them to go ahead."

At that point the nurse called back and said, "Aren't you going to come? It seems like you really should be here." At this point, becoming outraged, Mrs. Jones said, "We've just been trying to find out what's going on. Of course we're going to come. We'll be there in fifteen minutes."

When the parents arrived at the hospital, the nurse immediately began to lecture them on how they did not know the appropriate procedure and shouldn't parents be a little bit more caring about what goes on? Mr. Jones, who happened to be a professor of health and medical care systems, was outraged at the notion and wanted to file a complaint. He looked for the patient representative at the hospital, but there was none.

Troubleshooter Actions   There was no one on duty at 9:00 P.M. Saturday night to take the complaint. Fearing retribution or poor service or both, the parents did not complain. Instead, they waited until their son was clearly all right, then wrote to the chief executive of the hospital. Meanwhile, they told many people of their bad experience at the hospital and about their inability to complain.

Troubleshooter action would have helped, but there was none in this case.

Case 11: A Prisoner's Complaint

The Complaint   Henry was a twenty-one-year-old inmate in a county prison with not much experience in correctional institutions. When he first arrived in the prison, the guard ordered him to clean his cell three times as part of the "welcoming initiation." The young inmate gave him some wise backtalk and refused to do it. Following that opening incident, the guard began a series of subtle and not-so-subtle harassments of veiled threats, denials of opportunity for recreation time in a couple of instances, and references to what could happen to him in the prison environment. After several weeks, the young inmate realized he had made a major error in the prison culture. He wanted to complain about the way he was treated. He went to the prison ombudsman to file a complaint, fearing harassment or even threats to his safety if he talked to the warden.

Troubleshooter Actions The prison ombudsman listened to the problem with sympathy and understanding. He suggested the inmate try to handle it himself by toleration and no response (hoping the harassment would just extinguish itself since it produced no return from the inmate). The ombudsman also suggested that he (the ombudsman) take the complaint to the warden to initiate a general "meet and discuss" with guards (of that unit first, then other units) over inmate harassment. At this point, there would be no direct action with the guard in question. The inmate was to report progress every other day and to alert the ombudsman immediately if the harassment became stronger. This was considered a first action, to be followed quickly with stronger action if needed.

Case 12: A Citizen's Complaint

The Complaint Sam Johnson lived on a well-traveled, somewhat rural, road which was rapidly developing as a main route to a number of new housing developments. Following one particularly hard winter, a rather substantial pothole opened up on the road. Sam decided that he would call the department of transportation. He informed the department that the pothole was both substantial in size and potentially dangerous, because there were several trees quite close to it on one side of the road. Somebody veering to avoid the pothole or going through it and losing control would go immediately into a tree. Sam filed several complaints with the department of transportation, but it appeared there was some dispute over whether it was a county road or a state road. No one would clarify who had the responsibility.

After some weeks of trying to sort it out, Sam decided to see if there was someone who could help him get the problem resolved, an effort that he thought was in the interest of public safety and good citizenship.

He called on the department of transportation's troubleshooter for assistance.

Troubleshooter Actions The troubleshooter took the details of the location and who had been contacted and told Sam she would get back to him in the next several days. The troubleshooter called the streets unit to find out if they knew of the problem and whether corrective action was to be taken. Although it was near a juncture with a county road, it was clearly state responsibility. The unit cited general work load problems and denied knowing of the complaint. The troubleshooter cited the need for quick action and asked if senior management should be involved. The unit director replied that it could be repaired in the next several days but would not specify when. The troubleshooter suggested that would be okay but made a note to follow up, assuming she would have to do so. Case—open.

Case 13: A Welfare Recipient's Problems

The Complaint In one state, welfare recipients received their check by mail. One mother with two small children and a missing husband was having difficulty ensuring that the welfare department send her checks to the correct address. It was true that she had to move several times in order to arrange suitable living arrangements because of the breakup of her family. However, the checks were repeatedly sent to the wrong address.

After all the necessary change-of-address forms were filed, the checks first went to the wrong address, an old address, and were returned to the department. The next set of checks went to another previous address, but did not arrive until a significant time later, since they were forwarded by a friend who helped informally. The third time she attempted to correct the problem, they got her address right but spelled her name wrong and she was unable to cash the check. After repeated calls to the welfare department (the bureau of names and addresses or some such department), she called on the troubleshooter for assistance.

Troubleshooter Actions   The troubleshooter was able to get the facts by telephone—correct name, address, and to whom she talked. The woman had to receive a corrected check immediately. After identifying the correct department, she requested a quick correction from a staff member. The response was a series of reasons why it would take days, if not a week. The troubleshooter said that would not do. She told the staff member she would need a meeting and would call back in several hours. The troubleshooter next called the unit director and explained the situation, including the need for immediate action. The director offered one view of immediate that was not acceptable. The troubleshooter and the director agreed to meet with the complainant at 4:00 P.M. that afternoon to resolve the problem—to secure a new check. The troubleshooter called the welfare recipient to tell her to come in.

Case 14: Complaint from a Gas Company Customer

The Complaint   Mr. Davidson had just purchased a property from the estate of an elderly woman. The woman heated the three-story house, now converted to apartments, with gas heat. Mr. Davidson wanted to rent out the apartments and began to do so, incorporating payment for the heat in the rental amount. He retained responsibility for paying the heating bills.

As the winter began, the gas company sent a bill based on the estimated previous year's cost, which appeared to Mr. Davidson to be astronomical. On calling about the cost, he found that the elderly woman was apparently a very heavy user of gas and kept the building very warm. Mr. Davidson explained to the utility company that he would make radical changes in gas use, and through insulation and construction, would be reducing the gas bill substantially. The gas company said that it would read the meter on a regular basis.

After two months, the gas company indicated that it had not been able to read the meter but again submitted a very high bill. Mr. Davidson suggested that its representative come out to read the meter and agreed to meet him or her there. The meter reader never showed up at the agreed time. Mr. Davidson complained.

Meanwhile, the gas company sent another bill, this one based on the previous year's heat cost, and demanded payment. Mr. Davidson said that he would not pay until they got a real reading of the correct amount of gas usage under his new ownership. The gas company threatened to cut off heat to the facility.

After attempting to negotiate a solution with the payment collections department, Mr. Davidson called on the troubleshooter for assistance.

Troubleshooter Actions   The main troubleshooter action from the company's customer representative involved scheduling and attending a meeting of the customer with representatives from the meter reading group and billing department. As facilitator in a tense meeting, the customer representative was able to negotiate a time and place to read the meter—that afternoon. He was also able to establish a regular time for meter reading that was to be passed on to the tenants and posted in the apartment. He expected all parties to honor the solution—old bills and collections letters were destroyed—although the billing and collections people were not fully pleased. Neither was the customer, since no apology was directly made. All agreed that further time on the problem was not useful.

The customer representative made a note to follow up.

Summary

The customer-involved cases are much like employee problems. Often they are people-based conflicts with the core action being confrontation and resolution meetings. Often the troubleshooter does not have a sense of whether the solution was immediately and permanently successful. In short, the cases lack closure.

The sample cases cited provide a sense of the nature of troubleshooter work—varied and interesting. What is probably not apparent from these brief descriptions is the high level of emotional involvement in each case. The cases are stressful and loaded with conflict. The seeming ease of resolution is only an artifact of the telling. Most dispute resolutions are hard, involving change for both people and organization; neither is willing to change easily.

These case examples reflect the work of formal troubleshooters, those officially recognized by title and position. They are also representative of the informal troubleshooter's caseload. This means that these cases are also likely to be the ones addressed by human and employee relations managers, executive assistants, sales representatives, and trusted senior people who have "adopted" the role. The degree of formality with which the problem solver solves the problem is the differentiating element between formal and informal troubleshooters, not the nature of the case.

The cases are representative of the caseload of both consumer and employee troubleshooters. The types of actions taken—formal and informal fact finding, meeting arrangement, personal counseling, communication to senior management—are representative response actions of all troubleshooters. Some troubleshooters are concerned with products and services, others with work and work-related performance.

Troubleshooters for both employees and customers must successfully solve problems. How the organization tracks the troubleshooter's performance is the subject of Chapter Nine.

9

Evaluating and Controlling
the Problem-Solving Program

It is often assumed that once managers are exposed to the concept of troubleshooting, they immediately recognize its value. However, in discussions of program start-up, managers quickly indicate how afraid of the concept they really are. Executives and managers express concern that the troubleshooters will "get out of control." They fear that troubleshooters will use the power of their position to stir up problems and create conflicts, manufacturing a steady stream of headaches for vice presidents, senior management, and supervisors as well as for technical people such as physicians and engineers. For this reason, this chapter discusses control of the troubleshooter, and how the characteristics of controls relate to the nature of the problem-solving job itself.

To systematically explore troubleshooter control issues, we will rely on the work of a well-known management commentator, Peter Drucker. Many readers are already familiar with Drucker's approach to management control. His writings on the nature and characteristics of management control can be related quite nicely to the troubleshooter function. Before we introduce his views, consider the patient's husband, Donald Johnson, in this chapter's opening case.

The Patient Sues?

Donald Johnson's wife was ill for several months before she was diagnosed as having cancer. Since she was sixty-seven, he realized it would be an uphill battle from the start, but when she died in six weeks he was both shocked and angry. He wondered about the delay in the diagnosis and about the treatment uncertainty. When he tried to telephone his wife's physician three or four times, the doctor was too busy to return his calls. His son told him, "If he won't talk to you on the phone, he'll talk in court. Sue him, Dad." Should he?

Donald Johnson's son wants him to sue the doctor, but Mr. Johnson heard that there was a patient representative at the hospital. He contacted the patient representative (a troubleshooter for hospital customers) to present his case just to see if she could do anything before he went to his lawyer. She listened carefully to the case, asking for details—as much as Mr. Johnson could remember. She thanked him for coming, saying she would investigate and get back to him within a day or two.

Some hospital CEOs and some physician medical staff chiefs would be very nervous about this exchange and the "investigative action" and "interaction" it would generate. Just how is the patient representative's performance controlled? Troubleshooter controls are derived from control thinking in general.

Drucker begins a presentation in his book *Management* (1973, pp. 496-497) by identifying three characteristics of management controls:

1. Controls can be neither objective nor neutral.
2. Controls need to focus on results.
3. Controls are needed for measurable and non-measurable events.

A discussion of each of these characteristics will reinforce the preceding commentary on the nature and function of troubleshooters and will introduce the various ways of controlling the troubleshooter.

First, controls are not objective or neutral. The work of a troubleshooter cannot be objectively assessed in a pure scientific sense. To begin with, certain constraints are built into the troubleshooting function itself. For example, most troubleshooters and ombudsmen are not allowed to encourage the employee or customer to hire an attorney and sue the company. While this might be an eventual result of a failure to resolve the problem, management is not interested in increasing the amount of litigation it faces. Management relies on the troubleshooters to solve the problem, especially including a solution without litigation. Limits on the encouragement to use the courts demonstrate that the troubleshooter is not there strictly for the benefit of the employee or customer (for example, as an advocate pursuing an adversarial relationship with the organization). Instead, both organization and employee or consumer are jointly represented by the troubleshooter, who attempts to maximize the gain while minimizing the loss for each party. Taking the physician to court cannot retract a death, but compassionate explanation and listening will ease the pain.

What does this mean from the perspective of the goals and values of the organization and the approach of management? It essentially says that the troubleshooter is free to explore solutions within the limits allowed by that managerial style. In other words, the scope and depth of control are determined by the nature of the organizational culture. For example, a corporate ombudsman operating in an autocratic managerial culture would be unlikely to have very much freedom to work in. But when a corporate ombudsman is free to openly pursue various resolutions to a problem (regardless of the issues raised for the executive team), this indicates that the managerial approach is both participative and open, not autocratic and closed in nature. Or in some hospitals, any patient/physician conflicts are open to confrontation and resolution, while in others, complaints are quickly smoothed over or repressed if a key physician could be "bothered" by the problem.

Second, in Drucker's view, controls must focus on results. This means that a troubleshooter's job is to solve problems, not to create data systems or to establish committees, groups, and interdepartmental conversations. Organizations are not interested in how much paper is generated in terms of complaint reports, progress reports, follow-ups, and recommendations. Instead they value individual and organizationwide problem solving (in such a way that it does not recur either easily or often). This results orientation tends to hold down the amount of bureaucratic control type of paperwork in most troubleshooter programs. Many troubleshooters do not prepare monthly performance reports, for example. Government agencies with statutory authority are often the exception.

Third, the control system must address both measurable and nonmeasurable events. This is perhaps the most difficult control area. For instance, in the literature on ombudsman work, there is some attention given to the nature and distribution of complaints and the analysis of data on those complaints. However, there is almost no discussion relative to the subtle and indirect effects that the ombudsman has on the organization, an evaluation design problem (Danet, 1978; Ziegenfuss, 1985c). Evaluations, research, and management assessments do not often address these questions. What are the attitude, motivation, and expectation changes generated as a result of the troubleshooter's presence? What does it mean for an individual employee when he or she knows that the organization cares enough to create a problem-solving position filled by a person sincerely committed to listening to employee concerns and to fair treatment? These are challenging evaluation subjects and a part of the problem of management control of this work.

There is a widespread belief by people in the troubleshooter business that the greatest impact of their efforts is generated by the indirect and subtle influences of their existence in the organization, regardless of whether they troubleshoot for employees in industries or consumers in hospitals. This means, however, that the most difficult aspect of the field—observing and controlling troubleshooters' unseen effects—is the most important!

A fearful executive might ask, "How do I know that the troubleshooter is not using fear, intimidation, and insecurity to solve problems?" While to some extent this concern about an "out of control" troubleshooter is legitimate, most troubleshooters and ombudsmen will tell you that it is not very long after the use of any of these techniques that the whole organization seems to know that they have been "leaned on." Power plays are necessary (and legitimate) for solving a few problems in a few situations. But continued and ongoing use of strong-arm tactics will quickly result in the troubleshooter's rejection by the organization. This is because the helping orientation of the troubleshooting mission has been converted into a policing one. These tactics are successful in a few division or department conflicts, but ongoing use would quickly diminish and eventually eliminate an ability to function effectively as a problem solver.

In summary, it seems that the control of subtle and indirect impacts that the troubleshooter has should not be of any greater concern (with regard to documentation) than control of the measurable aspects of the job. The level of subtle and indirect effects is easily known by the informal system and will be quickly communicated to the troubleshooter and to management. Trouble-shooters will get fewer cases to handle and management will get an "earful of anger" if strong-arm tactics are used.

Troubleshooter Control System Specifications

Drucker has identified specifications for managerial controls. These specifications translate into a guideline for designing controls, enabling us to identify the characteristics of management's troubleshooter control system. Managerial control systems must meet the following specifications. The system must be

- economical
- meaningful
- appropriate
- congruent
- timely
- simple
- operational

How do designers of a troubleshooter program address these control characteristic questions? In one sense, they represent elements of a model troubleshooter control system. How do they relate to a case? Consider an incident with one employee.

The Boss's Home Repairs

Joe Roberts had been a maintenance worker at a school for just two years. At age fifty-four, he had tired of general construction and found he could not handle the work load as easily as before. He had been delighted to get the maintenance job. When his boss asked him to spend several days doing work at the boss's house, he was shocked. He was afraid to say no for fear of being fired. He was also afraid to do the work for fear of being fired. What could he do?

Keep this case in mind as we examine the elements of the control system, asking the question, how do we effectively control troubleshooter work and troubleshooters?

Economical Controls must be economical. In management circles, there is a significant debate about how elaborate and formal a control system needs to be. This is true for troubleshooters as well. Do we want troubleshooters filling out contact reports, progress reports, complaint reports, follow-up reports, monthly reports, quarterly summary reports, six-month reports, and year-end reports? Or do we want them solving problems, spending very little time on documentation? Obviously some balance is in order; the question is whether it should be in the direction of higher cost and formality or informality and economical operation.

Troubleshooters such as employee assistance counselors and ombudsmen debate how much written documentation should be retained. Currently there is no consensus on this subject. There are clusters of people both for and against documentation that would be part of a monitoring and control system. There are a large number of troubleshooters who feel that the chief executive officer knows firsthand about the quality and success of the work. Conversely, CEOs also learn almost immediately about failure—the employee or customer conflict continues and escalates. The complaints from customers and employees are often significant and sensitive. When they blow up, they do so with loud bangs, not little ones. Impending litigation from a deceased patient's husband is not a trivial situation, nor is the potential suicide or sabotage of an employee.

Because of intimate CEO knowledge, formal troubleshooter controls tend to be relatively light. There are some industry differences, however. In the public sector, for example, trouble-shooter controls tend to be fairly extensive. Accountability is a notable and often-used buzzword in public systems—appropriately so. Public sector troubleshooters such as statutory-based ombudsmen and public advocates need to keep extensive case and report materials to identify the nature, volume, characteristics, and outcomes of the complaints they handle. The control system for public sector troubleshooters is therefore quite extensive, elaborate, and time-consuming, contrary to Drucker's principles of control. Private sector corporate ombudsmen do keep some records and files, but pressures to develop elaborate reports to meet monitoring requirements are not prevalent.

Joe Roberts' problem of working on the boss's house is illustrative. In a public agency, the "official troubleshooter" would need to complete a form outlining the complaint, the facts of the case, who was talked to, what records if any were reviewed, and the outcome of problem intervention. This might be written up in a one- to three-page report linked by case number to a formal filing system. A private sector corporate ombudsman might investigate the problem, press the supervisor to drop his request, and record nothing, feeling that the problem was solved or eliminated. The extent of formal control, in terms of documentation, is very different in the private sector. Private systems depend less on formal controls open to future review. Some would say control without documentation is nonexistent—but economical. No system equals no burden.

Meaningful Controls must be meaningful. The troubleshooter and the chief executive officer must identify the significant results of job performance. What would the troubleshooter use to enable the executive to know that he or she is doing the job (the management-by-objectives model)? Many aspects of the troubleshooter work process are potentially measurable. There are a few key elements that help the executive determine whether the troubleshooting is vigorous and effective. The following are sample measures:

- complaint contact volume: how many
- actual complaint volume: contacts that are fully processed complaints
- nature of the complainants: age, sex, race, organizational distribution, job position

- nature of the complaints: type and subject
- primary list of outcomes: organizational responses categorized (for example, actions taken; policy/procedure changes, decision reversals)

This relatively short list can be used on a frequent basis (such as monthly), to help an executive determine whether or not the troubleshooter function is well received in the organization. For example, are many complaints filed—ten complaints a day or only five a month?

The chief executive officer is able to determine from the location data whether complaints are being filed by members throughout the organization, or whether only certain types of employees in selected divisions or departments are filing. Customer groups can be tracked by product and geographical location. Additionally, a "general sense" of the achievements by the troubleshooter is revealed by the outcomes data. This is really the bottom line, the benefits of troubleshooter work. Are the complaints successfully resolved (yes or no in direct terms), and what were the outcomes (restitution, changed policy, personality conflict resolution)?

By concentrating on volume, nature of the complaints, nature of the complainants, and outcomes (four fairly simple measures), the chief executive officer should have enough meaningful data for control of the troubleshooter function. In management-by-objectives terms, these can be considered four key results areas for the troubleshooter. The chief executive officer can dispense with the lengthy progress reports, data about investigations held, who was contacted, hours of the day contacted, and so on that are used in some public programs. A "lean" control-reporting system avoids this seemingly endless supply of very detailed facts about the process of troubleshooter work, ensuring time to support the people orientation of the job and the problem solving.

Appropriate   With the third characteristic, Drucker asks how we know whether the controls concern the significant aspects of troubleshooter work. Do the data collected and the controls in total address the critical aspects of the job? Can a judgment be made about the match between the performance of the troubleshooter and the objectives? One example here is that instead of simply counting the number of complaints per month or per year, one might begin to distinguish between the number of *significant* complaints. This acknowledges that complaints have "differential potential damage" to the organization—sabotage at a defense plant manufacturing army tanks versus Joe Roberts' dilemma over his supervisor's home repairs. If significant potential damage is threatened, that becomes a priority. A threat to kill a supervisor is more critical than an inappropriate transfer. Common sense says that threats may take on more importance than policy and procedure questions that may come in greater volume but that, even if not addressed, have lower potential for damage. A complaint about a smoking violation in the hospital is important, but far less so than the death of Donald Johnson's wife.

This requires a deeper understanding of the nature of the complaints. In some troubleshooter programs, a category entitled *litigation potential* is used. This measure "flags" the potential for litigation as a critical system control element. This can be a simple judgment measure—high, neutral, or low potential. Scanning this data enables the supervising manager to determine whether or not the troubleshooter is working with significant complaints and may assist the troubleshooter with time management.

An alternative to "formal data review" is a simple "meet and review" meeting with the CEO. A quick presentation of the case topics usually is sufficient to determine significance informally and without extensive paper requirements.

Congruent Congruency concerns whether the control measures used to gauge troubleshooter performance really do relate to the nature of the work. For example, in order to consider a successful resolution of 85 percent of the complaints over the course of a year (a high level) to reflect excellent troubleshooter performance, the nature of the cases must be taken into account. Were they cases that were very difficult with high litigation potential? Or were they cases that were relatively easy to resolve, primarily involving information and education for the work force or for consumers?

This congruency question relates to the key results. Do the control measures reflect the goals of the program? One customer relations troubleshooter may spend a long time "listening" to dissatisfied customers. At the end of the sessions, customers are no longer as angry, just because someone would listen. Their problems are not solved with just listening, however. Nor is the organization's development fostered. Action must be taken by employees and managers. Knowledge of the extent and nature of these follow-up actions is critical to determining whether troubleshooters are correctly addressing both organizational and individual problems.

Donald Johnson's dispute with the physician who treated his wife is an example. The physician would not listen—a problem the patient ombudsman can easily solve by listening. But that does not address the more fundamental problem of doctor/patient relations that may be present, if this one case is a reliable indicator of a widespread orientation. If no follow-up action is taken, the data relating to number of patients listened to can be very misleading. Listening is necessary but not sufficient for the full troubleshooter job, in other words.

Timely How frequently are the controls reviewed? How often does the chief executive officer meet with the troubleshooter? This is also the question of how frequently the CEO *should* be meeting with the troubleshooter to check performance. Drucker (1973) notes that quick and constant control can be destructive to the work process. But in the case of the troubleshooter's ability to resolve problems, performance review should be ongoing. Troubleshooters must be in touch with the executive to whom they report, whether it is the CEO or a senior vice president. Reports are not needed. Regular face-to-face discussions about progress on significant cases are sufficient to determine performance. With the significance of the cases, the risk of delayed review and/or inattention is too great.

The timeliness issue is an absolute mandate with regard to some cases. All troubleshooters, like other employees, sometimes fail. Lack of timely control combined with a low level of executive involvement in selected cases could be disastrous for the organization. In our case examples, Joe Roberts could sue for wrongful termination or Donald Johnson could press for a malpractice award. The supervising executive must be involved on an ongoing basis; that is, a shorter control time span rather than a longer one is desirable not only for performance but because a terrific need for information exists with regard to volatile cases.

There is another point about timeliness of controls: the necessity of keeping executives in touch with the problems in the organization. Timeliness is tied to the fundamental organization development purpose of troubleshooting. To the extent that executives are distanced from the nature and volume of complaints in their units, departments, and divisions, they have reduced their ability to create timely responses to organizational problems. A time lag between complaints filed and response must be avoided.

This rule also applies to the timeliness of the controls. Limited communication between supervising executive and troubleshooter is a sign that controls are weak. There may be an "implied subcontracting" of the organization's problems to the troubleshooter. This is especially discomforting because sensitivity to the organization's status—including individual and unit problems—is a starting assumption for the success of a trouble-shooter program. And subcontracting responsibility for unit problems to the troubleshooter is one of the great fears cited by executives in resisting program development.

Consider the cases involving Joe Roberts' awkward situation and Donald Johnson's concerns about his wife's medical treatment. Who would want to work in or purchase goods or services from an organization with a CEO who does not care about these kinds of problems? Timeliness of control is inseparably linked to ongoing concerns about people (employees and consumers), the most valuable organizational resources.

Simple Simplifying the control indicators and the proce-dure is central to the success of the control process. With trouble-shooting, there is the potential to create many complex documents to support the control system, as evidenced in some public agencies. For example, in reviewing public sector ombudsman programs, high levels of documentation and legalistic complexity seem to be descriptive of the control system. However, the adequacy of the controls is not guaranteed by the paperwork. The bureaucratic approach to the control problem is a "tree killing operation" (using the paper), which often does not result in very effective control at all. Simple control mechanisms should become elaborate over time only if there is a need for complexity. The temptation, especially with the capability of current management information systems, is to begin with the complex and move toward the simple only after disaster strikes in the form of an inability to manage the volume of information.

Operational Controls must be operational. Successful troubleshooters seem only infrequently to have gotten into trouble with their interpersonal interaction or their problem resolution behaviors. But there are cases in which the troubleshooters should have referred the cases to attorneys or to outside sources and avoided the problem altogether. For example, medical cases that are likely to lead to malpractice suits require legal consultation at the outset. In these cases, operational controls need to be in place to help both the troubleshooters and the executives they are responsible to monitor the work process.

This suggests a need to actually use the control system that is designed. Debates over the level of complexity and the need for simplicity are truly irrelevant if executives do not use the few indicators that do exist. It is much less important whether the design is comprehensive to a compulsive degree than whether the items defined for monitoring are regularly reviewed.

Summary

This chapter surveyed characteristics of the control system used to monitor the performance of troubleshooters by focusing on seven design characteristics. Is the control system economical, meaningful, appropriate, congruent, timely, simple, and operational? The best troubleshooting system is simple and direct, involving a close working relationship to a reporting superior—CEO or senior vice president. The nature and activities of the troubleshooter's job are personal and people-based, not bureaucratic and paper-oriented. The control system should reflect the basic nature of the work.

10

Bottom-Line Benefits
of Problem-Solving Programs

This chapter discusses the benefits of a troubleshooter program that were identified in a general sense in earlier chapters. What happens in the organization as a result of a troubleshooter's presence? For readers interested in productivity gains and the subsequent benefit to the bottom line, there are both direct and indirect troubleshooter contributions. Some effects of the troubleshooter's work are directly visible (for example, obvious conflicts resolved, litigation avoided), while other effects are hidden (such as those pertaining to human relations). The latter, the indirect benefits, are especially critical but often are not felt or recognized.

Travel Denial

Ms. Jensen had worked for the department for some sixteen years. A program she developed had recently received much national attention. She was invited to participate in a major national conference to present the program for the first time to a large audience of professional colleagues. She was delighted and felt honored at the invitation. The department would receive both public and professional recognition for its innovation. However, her request for travel time and expenses was denied without explanation.

In the case of Ms. Jensen's travel time and expense denial, troubleshooter action may quickly secure the required time and support—a visible and direct result. However, a means to complain and receive redress helps to build a corporate culture that pays off over the years. Ms. Jensen's past work and devotion were apparently disregarded by management when they made their decision, the equivalent of shooting oneself in the foot, that is, undercutting commitment and morale.

The description of troubleshooter benefits conforms to the view of the host organization as a system, or more specifically, as an interconnected set of five subsystems (Kast and Rosenzweig, 1985; Ziegenfuss, 1985a). Public and private organizations are defined as having five subsystems: a goals and values subsystem (culture), a technical subsystem, a structural subsystem, a psychosocial subsystem, and a managerial subsystem. According to this view of the nature of an organization, troubleshooters affect at least one and possibly all of the systems; that is, there are widespread benefits for the organization. Figure 7 (on the next page) illustrates the mapping of troubleshooter effects.

Goals, Values, and Cultural Effects

What are the troubleshooters' effects on the goals, values, and cultural subsystem of the host organization? In most organizations, from hospitals to manufacturers, the presence of the troubleshooter is symbolic of the corporate culture that the chief executive officer is trying to develop and maintain. An underlying assumption of a culture that includes a troubleshooter function is that complaints are to be brought to light, investigated, and responded to in an open, fair, and responsible fashion. In other words, the trouble-shooter is one means for reinforcing the desired cultural characteristics of openness and fairness.

For example, one can often hear a hospital CEO remark: "In today's competition-oriented business atmosphere, we are true believers in patient (customer) satisfaction." But when you ask whether the hospital has a patient relations manager or a patient representative, he or she responds, "No we don't—they create problems." The presence of a troubleshooter/problem solver would signify a commitment to the "desired" cultural elements. The belief is backed up by a position. Resources are committed—money

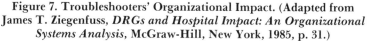

Figure 7. Troubleshooters' Organizational Impact. (Adapted from
James T. Ziegenfuss, *DRGs and Hospital Impact: An Organizational
Systems Analysis*, McGraw-Hill, New York, 1985, p. 31.)

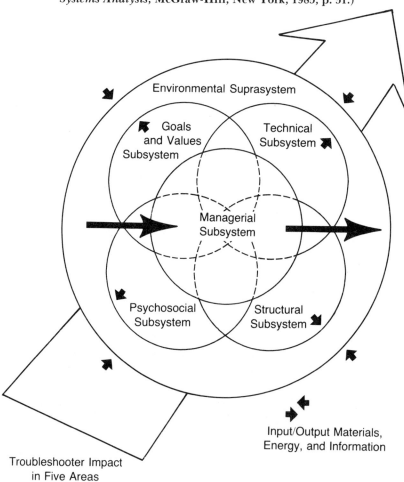

follows the rhetoric about increasing the quality of employee life
and quality of consumer life.

What does troubleshooting contribute to other aspects of the
organization's culture, including specific goals and values? One of
the critical values reinforced by the troubleshooter is the belief that
customer and employee viewpoints are needed and are listened to
by management and employees. Management values individual

participation, including the presenting of complaints. Management backs up this position with a means to help make it happen—the troubleshooter.

For example, many public agencies and private corporations promote the notion that employees are free to question any policies or procedures (a core value). This is thought of as great "internal public relations." But any benefits to be gained are lost if the questioning is in fact known (via the grapevine) to produce retribution or other difficulties for the questioners.

This is illustrated by the following typical case. Professor Watson objected to the bureaucratic handling of contracts, to the insensitive dismissal of student registration problems, and to poor facilities support. In return, he found resistance to his deserved promotion and proposed sabbatical.

Suddenly the complainers' rewards are reduced, their policy positions attacked. Few questioners keep going with that kind of "reinforcement." The cultural value of openness is demolished.

A related goal is the promotion of open communication among corporate participants—employees and consumers. The troubleshooter's abilities and responsibility for encouraging communication about complaints fosters dialogue in troubled areas, using communication as a first step to resolution. Moving between upper and lower levels of the organization and across management areas, troubleshooters clear channels demonstrating communication openness. This open discussion eventually becomes a ritual, "a part of the way we do things around here."

Rituals may play a negative role, however. What employee is not familiar with the ritual of simulated problem solving? This is not actual problem solving, but a charade in which employee complaints are supposedly encouraged, confronted, and responded to. This ritual is a hypocritical process in which the real activity is often a transparent attempt at internal smoothing over. The organization considers the problem-solving process to be a ritual that it must adhere to for employee public relations reasons but that is not designed to have actual effects. In short, it is not used to address problems within the organization. A response to Ms. Jensen's travel denial would be, "Sure you can file a complaint—talk to your manager, then personnel." The expectation is that the complaint will be "buried" by personnel or by the process, or by the inherent intimidation of lawyers. A process exists, say the defenders, empty as it may be.

Along with rituals as an indicator of culture, there are rites of passage up the organizational ladder. In many organizational cultures, one rite of passage involves acquiring an ability to tolerate unpleasant experiences. Management actions—transfers, policy conflicts, cutbacks, product eliminations—cause significant discomfort to employees at all levels. This rite of passage to the top requires an ability to take one's lumps and watch fellow employees take their lumps without grumbling about unfairness and damage to both person and organization. While this may be useful for developing management ability to overcome setbacks, it does not help to resolve pressing problems.

The presence of the "grin and bear it" philosophy is part of a developmental process that creates the "heroes" of the organization, leaders who have a negative attitude toward complaining. But this raises the question of who the heroes of the organization really are. Are they the senior executives, department heads, and supervisors who look the other way when problems develop, ignore them as long as possible, or smooth them over without significant confrontation? Or are the "heroic" managers problem-confronting and problem-solving in outlook and action? The presence of a troubleshooter is evidence that the organization wants management, employees, and consumers to identify and confront problems. From this perspective, the heroes of the organization are not the managers and employees who grin and bear it, ignoring problems as long as possible, but are activists who move quickly to understand and address all types of employee and customer complaints in the organization. Therefore, one underlying troubleshooter contribution is to help create new management heroes.

How do rites, rituals, and heroes combine to support a cultural network? All organizations from hospitals to manufacturers to banks have a set of goals, values, rituals, and heroes that define and maintain the cultural network (Schein, 1985; Deal and Kennedy, 1982). This "in group" (heroes) in good organizations understands that *all* companies have problems and that they must be addressed directly and fairly. The presence of a formal troubleshooter, a corporate or public ombudsman, means that this cultural network includes someone who continually reminds the members of the group of the necessity to confront and resolve organizational problems.

For example, how is Ms. Jensen's travel denial to be handled? Is it treated as an isolated incident unrelated to morale and long-term human resource development? Or is it treated as a single problem with potentially complex positive benefits to be derived from successful resolution? Using this single incident as a lead to understanding organization behavior sets the problem up as an organizational learning opportunity.

What effects does a troubleshooter have on culture change? In the 1980s many experts have begun to stress the usefulness of changing the organizational culture to continue the organization's development. What impact does the troubleshooter have on this process?

In one organization, the troubleshooter is assisting in moving the company *away* from an autocratic "I don't give a damn about the people or their problems," "Productivity is all important" approach. The new culture is one that believes that "People are our most important resource" and "One way to protect this resource is to identify, understand, and address their complaints." In this company, the troubleshooter is part of a management effort to change the culture. In cases such as this, troubleshooters help change a culture that is closed and autocratic to one that relies on and maintains open communication. They are communication agents that subvert autocracy and closed-system thinking.

In summary, troubleshooters make a significant contribution to the development and maintenance of the organizational culture, helping to change the culture when that is the agenda. They help to develop new "heroes"—managers and employees who fairly and justly deal with complaints in the work force. Troubleshooters foster a cultural network whose membership criteria include (1) a belief in open communication, (2) the assumption that all organizations have problems, and (3) the realization that the most useful approach to complaints is to identify and deal with them promptly and directly.

Technical Effects

What is the troubleshooter's effect on the technical subsystem of the organization? The technical subsystem comprises all of the inputs, activities, and outputs that are regarded as the primary work of the organization in a given industry, for example, health care, transportation, banking. In hospitals, this is the medical and health care services; in the automobile industry, it is the engineering processes used to create automobiles.

How do complaints affect the resources used in the technical process? For example, complaints from one sales unit indicate that information from the marketing group regarding preferences for automobile model and style may not be sufficient to generate corrective action. But in combination with a complaint from the manufacturing division, poor customer preference data can be identified as a significant problem for operations. As a second example, an increasing number of complaints about alcohol abuse on the assembly line should alert managers that the manufacturing process may be exerting too much pressure on employees, or it may simply be too boring.

In other troubleshooter cases, employees and customers complain about the quality of products or services produced. These are complaints about the outputs of the technical work process. Some employees are fired as a result of technical system complaints (for example, the "whistleblower" cases). In aerospace projects, their complaining was viewed as disloyal and threatening to the defense department, to NASA, and to private corporations. An alternative view is that these employees are performing a service by sounding an alarm about technical process deficiencies. Rather than firing these employees, a good corporation—one concerned with maintaining an open culture as a means to quality and productivity—will use complaint data to identify trouble spots in the technical production of goods and services. The troubleshooter process helps the group to confront and address problems not with an adversarial intent but with a technical and organizational development orientation. Complaints filed by employees are viewed as one data source by which the programs, methods, and total technical processes of the corporation are monitored; that is, they represent a contribution to quality control (Ziegenfuss, 1985c).

One example was the complaint by an employee about a new computer system the chief executive officer had developed in the first year after his arrival at the company. The computerized management information system was a complete fiasco. Initial heavy-handed use of inaccurate data was fostering fear and anxiety, including cheating about sales targets met and antagonistic infighting among various departments. The employee was afraid to complain to his department supervisor who, he felt, would be afraid to complain to the vice president. Instead, the complaint was passed anonymously to the troubleshooter. The troubleshooter was able to follow up on this single complaint by conducting a brief investigation, pulling together supporting evidence that the system was flawed. Using diplomacy and trading on his relationship, he gave this information to the chief executive in a way that made the bad news seem at least partially palatable. Since the troubleshooter had a close and positive working relationship with the CEO, he was able to pass on the bad news without "getting the messenger killed" (as might have been the case with the employee or vice president). Here the troubleshooter was able to contribute to improving the work process in the corporation by breaking the communication blockage and by identifying a technical problem.

Troubleshooters contribute to maintenance and development of the technical work by

- acting as a transmitter and interpreter of the historical technical practices of the organization
- acting as a communication vehicle for informing management when technical errors appear
- helping to guard the confidentiality, ethics, and fairness of technical and scientific processes
- acting as a feedback mechanism for the technical personnel to inform them that applications are not complete or well prepared
- providing data for redesign and new design of technical outputs and the processes that create them

These are both regular and irregular, continuous and sporadic troubleshooter contributions.

Structural Effects

How does the troubleshooter affect the structure of the host organization? Structural chracteristics (developed by Daft, 1983) can be used to track this type of troubleshooter effect, examining formalization, specialization, standardization, hierarchy of authority, centralization, complexity, professionalism, personnel configuration. The examples cited are illustrative structural effects of troubleshooting. They may not be representative of a specific troubleshooter's duties, nor are they exhaustive.

Formalization Few persons in large organizations would dispute that most large organizations are formalized. Almost everything must be written and discussed, reviewed in meetings, and recorded in a file note. Formalization of private and public organizations has gone to such lengths that when conflict occurs, employees and customers are tempted to hire attorneys to help them through the complex bureaucratic systems. One benefit of troubleshooter presence is an alternative to this formality. Troubleshooters solve problems informally without using the often legalistic and bureaucratic procedures of large and small complaint systems. If an organization is less formal, the troubleshooter helps to keep informal problem solving alive. If in management's view the organization is regarded as too formal, troubleshooters can be a part of a cultural change process—a means by which informality and problem solving can be injected into the system.

Specialization Many commentators in technical and scientific fields have noted the phenomenal increase in specialization and the difficulties it causes in terms of cross-specialty communications. Troubleshooters are problem-focused linking pins between and within specialty groups, such as engineers, computer scientists, and physicians. The troubleshooter listens to and responds to concerns about specialists' work, or about the discontinuities in production processes that are causing problems for segregated specialists or employees. Specialists build walls around their areas, locking out either competing specialties or overlapping ones, creating barriers to communication. Troubleshooters help keep specialty communications open, becoming one means by which specialties can jointly address problems of mutual concern for which neither has independent responsibility.

Standardization   In the drive toward greater efficiency, major corporations and public agencies use standardization as the mechanism of choice. While standardization does promote efficiency, it often does so at the expense of individuality and innovation. Troubleshooters preserve some of this autonomy and freedom as defenders of individuality and innovation, particularly when employees or consumers are pressed by hostile political forces who insist there is one "best" way. This kind of standardization is a contributor to innovation blockages that are slowing down American leadership in creating new products and services.

At the same time, troubleshooters help to ensure that there is increased standardization in certain areas, for example, the fair treatment of customers and employees with regard to a wide range of policies and procedures from recruitment, to tranfer, to termination. In several of the cases cited, it was noted that some firings resulted from deviation from what was perceived to be "the way things are done around here," not poor performance. Standardization to increase fairness and justice for all employees in the organization is a most desirable goal, one supported by the troubleshooter.

Hierarchy of Authority   Many organizations operate with a hierarchy of authority that is rigid and controlling. The troubleshooter represents authority (see Chapter Five) but is sanctioned to bypass the hierarchy where needed. The hierarchy interferes with the communication of problems to executives because no one wants to tell the next level up about a problem. Executives with the power and influence to create change often do not know about the problems. Troubleshooters enable this authority hierarchy to function more effectively by establishing a bridge between levels.

Authority is intact but is no longer a barrier to a quick response to problems.

When sales quotas seemed too high for a sales group—they knew they were working hard in a competitive environment—they did not want to tell the regional supervisor or the vice president of sales. Certainly the desired behavior is open communication. But in a macho-type environment, fear of failure and not wanting to break the "can do" image causes resistance to providing feedback. The intent is not to have salespeople regularly use the troubleshooter for this purpose, unless there is no other option. It is better to use the troubleshooter than to let the problem exist without addressing it, however.

Centralization   There is a centralizing effect to trouble-shooter problem solving. Senior management may be centralizing problem identification—but not the problem solving itself. Problem-solving process responsibility and the responsibility for tracking patterns of problems (both within and between units) is now centralized in a person who reports directly to senior management. This enables a picture of the total organization's problem set to emerge as a first step toward taking appropriate corrective action.

Complexity   Troubleshooters work in complex organizations, such as hospitals, high-technology firms, major manufacturers. High complexity requires high levels of communication to overcome the difficulties in coordinating various units within the organization. Troubleshooters minimize the negative effects of complexity by targeting specific problems and solutions in this web of technical and social systems.

Complexity confronts employees and consumers right at the start of the problem action. "How do I find out where to go to file a complaint about this problem?" The troubleshooter is a "complexity reducer" acting to communicate concern (caring) and acting as a guide to assistance. Troubleshooters can cut through the complex policies, procedures, authority, and resistance to get rapid resolution. From an employee or customer perspective, that is a significant and valuable contribution to problem solving.

Professionalism   Troubleshooters increase professionalism. Professionals, both scientists with extensive credentials and employees who have had long years of experience and commitment on the job, increase their professionalism by honestly confronting and attempting to resolve problems. Do employees tell customers to "take a walk"? Are employees told to keep quiet? Professional values and beliefs require that employees and consumers must be able to voice their concerns. Professionals also know that the corporation benefits from free and open discussion of customer and employee complaints about the failures of various parts of the organization. In many ways this is part of the concept of professionalism—the willingness to listen, understand, and respond to complaints about goods and services sold.

Personnel Configuration   The presence of troubleshooters means that the personnel structure supports certain values, such as listening to employees' and consumers' complaints. Program start-up means that management believes that the structure must include a way of fostering problem-oriented communication and problem solving.

A troubleshooter is an indicator of structural flexibility. Troubleshooters are not classified as management or as production employees. They exist within the personnel structure to foster linkages between the two, without actually being a part of either.

Psychosocial Effects

This section reviews troubleshooter effects on the psychological and human relations system of the organization. The topics to be discussed are behavior patterns, motivation, expectations, needs, status and role systems, group dynamics, leadership, and power. In both direct and indirect ways, troubleshooters positively affect individual and group dynamics—people relations in the organization.

Behavior Patterns   Troubleshooters demonstrate problem-solving behaviors, provide evidence of how the culture values listening (sometimes a new behavior pattern), attempt to understand employee and customer concerns (perhaps a new behavior pattern), and address and resolve employee and consumer complaints (all too often a new behavior pattern). This is desirable organizational behavior, since it contributes to the quality of employees' working life and the quality of consuming life.

Motivation Troubleshooters increase motivation. They do so by supporting employees' beliefs that the organization cares about the problems employees feel need to be resolved in order to get on with the job. Demonstrating concern increases motivation. Anyone who has encountered unresolved problems—technical and personal—knows how they can undercut motivation. Good problem resolution for customers maintains customer loyalty and buyer motivation.

Expectations Troubleshooters create expectations. What do employees expect to happen as a result of the complaining? What happened before the troubleshooter program existed? If the expectation is that complaints are not likely to be addressed, understood, or listened to, employees begin to look the other way when they encounter barriers to quality and productivity. The presence of a troubleshooter suggests that the employee can expect the organization to listen, to investigate, and to act on their complaints. The expectation is that this corporation will remove barriers to quality and productivity. In fact, the corporation has established a means for doing so—the troubleshooter program.

For customers, the response is two-directional. If complaints are not addressed, they (1) take their business elsewhere, and (2) tell their friends about their "bad experience."

Needs Troubleshooters meet employee needs. One employee need is to be able to comment on and affect the workplace from policies to procedures and physical conditions. The troubleshooter is one means by which employees can meet their needs for control and power over their work environment.

Status and Role Systems Troubleshooters have high status because of their reporting relationship to top management. What status issue does this raise for employees and management? Because of the troubleshooter's high status, employees and managers who confront and address complaints increase their status. High-status troubleshooters have a status-enhancing effect by passing on to top management information about the good performance of problem-solving managers. At the same time, the official presence of a troubleshooter legitimizes a role that otherwise exists informally, since as we have seen, there are experienced employees acting as troubleshooters in most, if not all, organizations. When the troubleshooter role becomes a recognized part of the organization, this is evidence of the importance of this work and testimony to senior management's willingness to invest resources.

Group Dynamics Troubleshooters affect group relations when they act as mediators. There is a within-group effect when the troubleshooter acts as a third-party consultant to groups "at war." For example, in one corporation the manufacturing and sales departments cannot seem to effectively coordinate their schedules. The problem cannot even be discussed because of a personality conflict between the vice presidents in charge of both functions. In this case, the troubleshooter is a catalyst for change in the group dynamics and a mediator of an interpersonal dynamic that is a barrier to problem solving and productivity.

Leadership An executive decision to establish a trouble-shooter position demonstrates leadership by admitting that organizations of all kinds in all industries have problems and that these problems should be recognized and confronted. Leadership is not just rhetoric about problem solving but a willingness to expend resources.

Power Troubleshooters decentralize problem-solving power. Troubleshooters have freedom to engage all appropriate parties in conflict resolution. It is a "floating" power base with a capability to move to the problem site. Problem-solving power is not located only in the chief executive officer or the top of the management hierarchy.

This completes our review of the psychosocial impact of troubleshooting programs. What are the troubleshooter's effects on management?

Managerial Effects

In this section, the effect of troubleshooters on the managerial system is surveyed. We focus on five management activities: planning, organizing, developing, directing/leading, and controlling. How does the troubleshooter help to initiate, develop, and maintain these managerial activities? What contributions are made to the managerial work of the organization?

Planning Troubleshooters contribute to organizational planning by providing data for goal setting. They are part of an organizationwide data collection effort that helps to identify problem areas and needs within the organization that must be addressed by management. For example, they may hear increasing numbers of complaints about certain employee personal problems in one unit or location, such as alcoholism at a high-stress military base, for example. This data calls for further investigation to define the problem and to determine what kind of action should be taken. Complaint reports are part of the database for management planning.

This complaint database leads to a managerial "do list." Diagnosis, planning, action, and future evaluation of the status of a wide range of problem topics is required. Troubleshooters are agents and promoters of organizational learning. The organization is able to learn about its strengths and weaknesses by reviewing the complaint data. Weaknesses are to be addressed by individual vice presidents, department heads, and the chief executive officer in the following planning time period.

Organizing Troubleshooters also make a contribution to the organizational activity of management. This activity includes, for example, the design of an organizational structure, the selection of personnel and facilities, the acquisition of capital, and the creation of information systems. Troubleshooters help the management staff identify "organizing" weaknesses, such as personnel shortages, facilities with poor physical environments, and malfunctioning data systems. We saw earlier that complaints from employees indicated that one unit became so hot with deficient air-conditioning that productivity had dropped significantly. Employees were grumbling on a constant basis about the work environment. As a second example, consider a computer system problem. Management information systems have received increasing attention in the last ten to twenty years. They are now a mainstay for the modern corporation and are becoming increasingly used in public agencies. However, one continuing design challenge is on the people side: attitudes, motivation, group dynamics, and resistance. Troubleshooter complaint systems can provide insight into the work force. *Complaints are a management information system element targeted at people problems.* Since it is very hard to obtain this type of data, it is an extremely worthwhile component of the overall management information system.

Developing There are two ways troubleshooters contribute to the "developing" activity of management, one micro and one macro. At the micro level, the benefit is to the person holding the troubleshooter's job (see also Chapter Eleven). At the macro level, the benefit is in terms of the overall development of the organization. Each area requires brief discussion.

On the micro level, some private corporations are using the corporate ombudsman function as a training position for future management and human resources executives. Performing the troubleshooter-ombudsman job for a period of time

1. teaches the jobholder about the strengths and weaknesses of the organization
2. develops problem-solving skills
3. teaches the jobholder about the trade-offs necessary to achieve a negotiated consensus and a solution to difficult problems
4. exposes him or her to various aspects of operations throughout the organization through the process of complaint solving

To the extent that troubleshooters need to be fairly experienced before they take the position, individual development does not necessarily occur early in the career. It is perhaps best used as a developmental tool for someone in their early to late thirties. It could be used as direct preparation for more senior positions in personnel or human resources or in general management.

There is at least one model in which micro development does not really occur. In some organizations, the troubleshooter-ombudsman is selected because of his or her successful career in the organization, a career that is nearly complete (for example, by age fifty-five to sixty-five). This is the case with the ombudsman at the World Bank, for example (Tillier, 1987). The job may still contribute to individual development but not toward a future career.

On the macro level, development can occur in all of the systems mentioned in this chapter. The effect of the troubleshooter is an organizational development one, with implications for the goals and values, technical, structural, psychosocial, and managerial systems of the company. A successful troubleshooter program enables the organization to

1. test goal and value consistency
2. reinforce certain values
3. create heroes who address complaints
4. identify technical and structural weaknesses
5. test for strong people-problem areas, whether in production or management
6. develop management in all of the areas mentioned in this chapter (planning, organizing, developing, directing/leading, and controlling)

Troubleshooter programs, by bringing out, testing, and proposing solutions to organizational problems, are by their very nature an organizational development tool.

Directing/Leading Troubleshooters also support the management activity of directing and leading the organization. How? First, they support management activity through problem resolution. Few managers would disagree that a significant amount of time is used up by problem resolution. In effect, some of this time consumption is delegated to the troubleshooter.

At the same time, the delegation allows the troubleshooter to assist in the interpretation of directions and leadership goals that management presents but which may not be communicated clearly. This goes back to the question of the core nature of the trouble-shooter's function and its involvement with communication. When management provides both direction and leadership, many employees (through no fault of their own and perhaps through limited fault of management) have further questions about the organizational future, about specific policies and procedures, and generally about the way in which the organization works. When these are significant, troubleshooters hear them, passing on to management the need to clarify them.

Additionally, the troubleshooters facilitate interaction that is necessary to get the direction and leadership points across. Often the conflicts that result between departments, subgroups, or individuals concern the new directions that management is promoting. The communication required for complaint finding and resolving supports management leadership.

Controlling   Last, troubleshooters are a type of control mechanism, in that the program is used to monitor problem identification and resolution. It is a performance review tool for management. Clearly a unit with many complaints must be examined, or questions relating to productivity and quality of working life will go unanswered.

It is worth noting that there is considerable debate among formal troubleshooters about the purpose and use of written complaint information. The field is divided with regard to the appropriateness of collecting and disseminating information. Many troubleshooters fear that this information will be used inappropriately and that damage to individual employees and managers—possibly including firings, career harm, and harassment—will result. Others feel that if the organization does not collect this information (in aggregate) to help itself identify problems, a valuable organizational intelligence resource is lost. As noted earlier, the author is in favor of data carefully collected and used.

Summary

This chapter has reviewed the impact of troubleshooters on various aspects of the organization, including the goals and values subsystem, the technical subsystem, the structural subsystem, the psychosocial subsystem, and the managerial subsystem. The review indicates that effects of troubleshooter programs are multidimensional and wide in scope. The final chapter will discuss the future of this approach to increasing productivity and the quality of working life.

11

The Future
for Problem-Solving Troubleshooters
in Organizations

The last chapter concluded the presentation of the purposes, work activities, and benefits of troubleshooters. Beginning with the pressures for program development, we reviewed considerations about work system design, the actual troubleshooter job activities, and such issues as authority and power. Additional topics included the troubleshooter as communicator of data from the "complaint information system," the performance controls on troubleshooters, and a review of the benefits of this work to the organization. This final chapter addresses five subjects: (1) the two primary purposes of troubleshooter programs, (2) the nature of the intervention that a troubleshooter initiates, (3) the "representativeness" of this view of the troubleshooter concept, (4) the benefits to the individuals holding troubleshooter jobs, and (5) the reasons for expected future recognition and growth of troubleshooting programs.

Purposes

By way of reviewing concepts and activities, what are the two main purposes of troubleshooter programs? Quite simply, they are designed to

- increase productivity
- increase the quality of working life and the quality of consuming life

One assumption of the model is that all organizations, both consciously and unconsciously, create barriers to productivity (and to the quality of working and consuming life). These barriers involve both technical elements (such as production processes) and human elements (including attitudes and behavior). The trouble-shooter works to reduce and eliminate them on a single-case level and on a systemwide "repeating-problem" level.

In one sales division, several young managers were uncertain about how and when they might begin to look for promotion to other management jobs. The troubleshooter arranged for one complaining sales manager to obtain career path guidance from human resources, which he received. The troubleshooter also passed on to the human resources director a suggestion about sales division career path orientation for young managers. Uncertainty about career future is one barrier to productivity—a barrier that translates into interference with sales.

The troubleshooter program is also designed to increase the quality of working life and the quality of consuming life. For employees, it provides an opportunity to communicate concerns, to question the organization's policies, and to feel that what they complain about will generate action. This increases the feelings and reality of employee control and commitment. If employees can make a difference, they feel good about the level of ownership of their place of work. It is literally in part theirs because they help to "redesign" it on a regular basis through communication of problems and dialogue about possible solutions.

The problems are both large and small—sabotage in a defense supplies plant, poor ventilation when office repainting is underway. Troubleshooter strength is based on recognition that both large and small problems have significant impact. Everyone recognizes the fears, anxiety, and negative impact associated with publicized sabotage. Too few managers recognize that the daily indignities of the workplace—inadequate heating and limited space, no opportunity for relaxation and socializing, poor team spirit—are also contributors to low quality of working life. Troubleshooters must respond to the significant and the seemingly less significant.

The softball competition case cited earlier in the book is a good example. Cheating in an off-hours softball game is in one sense not exactly life threatening to the corporation. However, the level of cheating and the need to do so even in a social game that does not really count may suggest something very profound about the corporate culture. Is there a need for companywide ethics and values discussions?

While quality of working life is a concept that is quite well known by now in management circles (Davis and Cherns, 1975), quality of consuming life is not. Who are the consumers/customers seeking a higher quality of consuming life? Based on published reports of troubleshooters at work, they would include patients in hospitals and nursing homes, college and university students, prison inmates, and buyers of all kinds of consumer products. The list is easily extended to nearly all businesses and industries. Few are without some form of troubleshooter identified as a customer relations specialist or representative. After all, customers want to believe they are buying quality products and services, and they want action when they have complaints. A company that listens, learns, and responds to customer problems is one that over time creates a high quality of consuming life for its customers.

Intervention

The purposes of troubleshooting are now clear—increased productivity and improved work life and/or consumer life quality. How are these goals achieved? Do the required changes involve adaptations to the technical and managerial work or to the people side of the organization? The term *intervention* links the troubleshooter program to organizational development strategies and methods (called *interventions*). As a form of management action, the troubleshooter contributes sociotechnical intervention. The key word is *sociotechnical*, meaning that actions of the troubleshooter are directed at both the social and the technical aspects of the organization (Trist, 1981; Davis and Cherns, 1975). This sociotechnical approach is a relatively new and increasingly popular way of addressing the joint social and technical design elements of any kind of organization, from manufacturing to education to health care. Major business management texts use its concepts as a basis for management problem diagnosis and follow-up action.

Many executives and managers forget that they cannot design

and develop new divisions or plants or make major changes in structures and functions without technical and psychological disturbance. When one company cut back from 60,000 to 35,000 employees over a several-year period, there was a flood of questions and complaints from employees. The topics included technical questions of work type and operating procedures and psychosocial questions of layoff fairness, open communication, and stress. Troubleshooters must respond to both types of questions.

Troubleshooters for customers have the same sociotechnical responsibility. For example, one woman was shocked to find that her husband died during a relatively routine hospital operation. She wanted desperately to find out what went wrong. The physician told her very little in a somewhat abrupt and arrogant manner. The woman sought the patient representative's help (the hospital troubleshooter) to obtain both technical information (about the failed treatment) and psychosocial support (sensitive caring during her grief).

The troubleshooter's work is aimed at correcting both social and technical design and operating difficulties that were either built in or are problems that have emerged. One employee troubleshooter may offer suggestions to employees in dealing with the stress of layoffs. The hospital troubleshooter may secure information on the technical treatment a patient received, having it presented again by the physician or a colleague. Troubleshooters, as good sociotechnical consultants, develop jointly optimized solutions to the problems—solutions that include factors of the social system (attitudes, morale, support) and the factors of the technical system (methods, procedures, rationale for results). This is consistent with and of great interest to engineers, for example, in high-tech industries where sociotechnical concepts are widely recognized.

The point is that troubleshooters should be flexible problem solvers who take both technical and social-psychological approaches.

Representativeness

How representative is the picture of troubleshooters that has been sketched in this book? Does it represent corporate and public ombudsmen, executive assistants, equal opportunity specialists, employee and customer relations representatives, dispute resolvers, and patient representatives? The answer is that it is very representative as a model and guide. It may not be precisely representative of a particular troubleshooter, of course. First, this perspective presents the primary design elements of the troubleshooter concept, with the emphasis on commonality across programs. The description reflected an effort to present the similarities based on the increasingly accepted systems view that jobs and programs have many design and activity elements in common across industries and organizational types. In addition, the description may not be very representative of a particular troubleshooter because all programs and people are somewhat unique. This qualification recognizes the individuality of human and organizational systems. A patient troubleshooter in a hospital works with patients, reports to a professional affairs executive, and receives perhaps $25,000 to $40,000 in salary. On the other hand, a troubleshooter at a major bank works with employees' problems, reports to the CEO of the bank, and may earn a salary of $75,000 to $100,000.

The design elements and activities of each troubleshooter program are numerous and can be varied within the conceptual framework, with the resulting combinations practically infinite. For example, troubleshooters can begin work early or late in their careers, can develop power because of established performance (or not), be friends with the CEO (or not), use a formal data system (or not). Each alternative means a slightly unique way of operating in that organization. This uniqueness, however, is not so great as to constitute a complete departure from the basic purposes and concepts. In short, there is a main concept and a set of procedures that are common to all. This description is thus in general representative of the troubleshooter concept.

Troubleshooter Development and Personal Benefits

The troubleshooter concept also benefits the individual in the troubleshooter's job. We can ask what the career development potential of troubleshooters is. The troubleshooter's function simultaneously contributes to the development of the organization and it trains future managers. The former was discussed in Chapter

Ten. The personal impact of the job on troubleshooters is our current topic.

Several years ago, I gave a lecture to a group of hospital CEOs about the purpose and use of employee and customer (patient) ombudsmen. As I finished the part of the presentation on employee ombudsmen, one CEO said, "Hey, that's the job I held before I became CEO. My boss said it was good training." His former boss used the post for his successor's development.

What we need to consider are two questions: (1) How promotable are troubleshooters to general management positions; (2) What points or job characteristics establish the "promotion potential" of the troubleshooter? To answer these questions, a set of the characteristics of "good" managers used by one graduate management assessment center is a helpful guide (Cutchin and Williams, 1984). According to this view, there are ten characteristics of a good manager: job knowledge, interpersonal skills, oral communication, written communication, supervisory skills, analytical skills, decision-making skills, planning, stress management, and creativity and innovativeness. It is important to note that these are not necessarily "the" perfect set of managerial qualifications for job success. Instead, they are used to identify and illustrate the promotion potential of the troubleshooter.

The topic of promotion potential is important for several reasons. First, there is a renewed interest in management's need to relate to customers and to employees (for example, see Peters and Waterman, 1982), a central troubleshooter purpose. Second, there is a related need for a management team that knows the intricacies of relations between employees and customers on the one hand and management on the other. And third, management is now attempting to increase productivity and to improve the quality of working life, key outcomes of troubleshooter work.

This analysis identifies areas of promotion potential to enable troubleshooters and their executives to engage in a dialogue about career options. Some points are obvious, others less so. Each characteristic is introduced with a definition.

Job Knowledge This is the work-related information developed through a combination of formal training and on-the-job experience that is used for job performance. Do troubleshooters know the business? The answer is clearly yes. Many troubleshooters are technical people with years of experience, including engineers in some companies, nurses in hospitals. They know their business intimately. Their promotion potential is very good, because in management jobs, you must know the business. Troubleshooters who do not know all about the business they are in when they start do know it a few years later. It is impossible to do troubleshooting without that knowledge. And over time, the complaints and problems enrich the troubleshooters' knowledge of the business and their organizations' roles and functioning. Problems are excellent teachers.

Interpersonal Skills These skills form the basis for work with people—not technology—and involve sensitivity to others, interest in and willingness to promote cooperation, verbal assertiveness, and the capability to give and take criticism. This one is obvious for troubleshooters, since interpersonal skills are absolutely necessary for mediating conflict. It goes without saying that troubleshooters should *not* be hired without interpersonal skills (neither should managers, for that matter). If they have been hired, they will not be successful in either a troubleshooter or a management job.

Some would argue that the essence of the troubleshooter's job is interpersonal. Some management analysts would also argue that the essence of management is interpersonal, particularly with the increasing use of task forces and the team approach. The promotion potential of the troubleshooter is therefore very strong in this area, especially if one realizes that after a few successful years, troubleshooters are interpersonal experts!

Oral Communication This of course involves the ability to talk with and understand others, including the ability to present instructions, information, and ideas clearly and concisely and also to listen. This is another primary aspect of the troubleshooter's job. Troubleshooters spend all day talking to customers or employees. They provide training, take part in orientations, and conduct meetings loaded with interpersonal conflict. The troubleshooter's job is *not* a nonverbal job. Promotion potential is addressed with the question—are there *any* nonverbal jobs in management? The strong verbal skills increase the troubleshooter's future value.

Written Communication   This is the ability to communicate the ideas and information of the organization in writing, for example through reports, letters, memorandums, and studies. Here the troubleshooter's work can involve reports that include outlining the complaint, the investigation processes and procedures, and the outcomes (although some troubleshooters do not write reports). The factual summaries of complaints are very similar to management memorandums presenting problem analyses. Written presentation skills are developed through repeated practice under strong staff scrutiny. The contribution to promotion potential derives from the troubleshooter's ability to write reports and memos.

Supervisory Skills   These could be described as the ability to lead by assuming responsibility and by asserting control. At first glance, the potential here seems to be lower than in the other areas, primarily because few troubleshooters have a staff of even six to ten plus. However, if supervision is considered in the sense of an ability to influence others, troubleshooters are in fact "supervising" many and diverse individuals in the complaint resolution process. This amounts to informal supervision, that is, responsibility for the persons involved without authority. It is management the "hard but effective way," requiring charisma and influence instead of an ordering or directing approach. This influencing ability makes the troubleshooter promotion potential strong, but less obvious than with the other points.

Analytical Skills   These emphasize the ability to identify and assess information used in management planning and decision making. Here we have another core activity of the troubleshooter's job—analysis of problems. How transferable this is depends on the nature of the complaints received. How analytical the troubleshooter needs to be depends on how complex the complaints are *and* on how supportive the organizational environment is (that is, its political complexity). A hospital troubleshooter may have a caseload filled with patient problems regarding bills and support services such as television and food. Or the patient representative could spend much time on treatment procedure and outcome cases that could lead to medical malpractice action. The latter are complex and difficult to analyze and resolve. In general, it must be said that the promotion potential is strong. Troubleshooting is analytical, as are many aspects of management, such as planning and problem analysis.

Decision-Making Skills   These include the ability to decide an issue in situations where an optimal solution is not possible, using information and judgment and a willingness to take risks with minimal guidance from senior management. The key term here is *optimal solution*. There are few, if any, solutions in either troubleshooter or management work that are perfect for all involved. Troubleshooters spend a considerable amount of time helping to create problem-solving solutions that benefit several conflicted parties. There is constant optimizing of the individual actor's positions in order to optimize the whole solution. The promotion potential here is very good, since there is much practice in helping others make decisions—a key management task. Troubleshooters encourage but do not force decisions, then must live with many persons' reactions to the decisions they help to forge.

Planning   We could describe this as the ability to create goals and to make decisions consistent with a task to be completed or a vision of the future. There are two aspects of planning that engage troubleshooters. First, there is an ongoing need to consider the alternative impacts of the complaint solutions in the future— the "planned change" that the solutions will create/initiate. Second, planning is a needed part of the management of the troubleshooter program, including the core activities of complaint taking, education, and consultation. There is promotion potential here, but somewhat less than in other areas. This is due mainly to the size of the operation and the need for limited planning work. Where there are several troubleshooters and a large program, promotability is higher, such as in planning for hospital trouble-shooter programs in a multihospital system.

Stress Management   This involves the ability to maintain emotional, mental, and physical health in crisis situations, implementing personal change when necessary. How many troubleshooters are not experts in stress management? Those without this expertise are likely to be unemployed. This is clearly because the job is very high stress. Those in it for any period of time must learn stress-coping skills. There is clear promotion potential here. Ask any chief executive officer how many management jobs have not been high stress in the past and how many will not be high stress in the next ten years. Simply put, stress management abilities are preparatory for higher management positions.

Creativity and Innovativeness   These traits are reflected in the ability to identify, develop, and carry out new ideas, programs, or projects. The troubleshooter's job depends on creativity and innovation. While some problems may seem routine and somewhat repetitive, solving them is a unique experience in every case. The people and situational contexts of employee/management and customer/provider problem solving demand individualized creative solutions. The strong promotional potential is based on the fact that creative problem solvers are always needed in management.

Promotion Conclusions   Characteristics of the management job were examined to determine the troubleshooter's promotion potential. Troubleshooters are customer- and employee-oriented. From this review, it seems that the role is also management-oriented in that it involves internal consulting and a contribution toward productivity improvement. Troubleshooters must have many of the skills and talents of managers. If they do not have them when they start, they soon develop them. Some organizations are already using troubleshooter positions for management training purposes.

Troubleshooters have high promotion potential for many management jobs, and in an age of increasing competition for customers and employees, CEOs should look to troubleshooters for new management talent. It will be worth the search, because troubleshooters know the personal and organizational benefits of putting customer and employee relations first, and they know how to do it.

The Future: Expansion of Troubleshooter Programs

Both public and private organizations will support the expansion of troubleshooter programs in the future. These programs are now beyond the start-up and critical mass stage; that is, they are established in very diverse industries, such as manufacturing, health, education, and corrections. Expansion is likely to occur for the following reasons.

First, our society is moving from a sole interest in hi-tech to a joint interest in hi-tech/hi-touch (Naisbitt, 1982). We are now engaged in a search for the means of maintaining and increasing the "touch," the human aspect. The troubleshooter is a personal problem solver working with people in high-technology business and industry. For example, a book describing patient troubleshooters in hospitals is called *Humanizing Health Care* (Hogan, 1980).

Second, the troubleshooter concept transfers across fields and organizations. It has already been tested in a wide range of businesses and industries and in many countries. Public agency ombudsmen (troubleshooters) have been at work for decades. Troubleshooters serve both employees (for example, in defense industries) and customers (such as patients in hospitals). In short, the concept can be applied to employees and customers in public and private organizations—in business, industry, government, and health care. The widespread testing and use is evidence of both the need for and the contributions of these programs.

Third, to follow up on this point about adoption by many companies and agencies, we can state that the concept is no longer experimental! Future expansion can be based on a wealth of experience that is public, private, and cross-cultural in nature.

Fourth, continuing growth in social system and organizational complexity will require some means for humanizing both society and individual organizations. Complexity and depersonalization from technology are increasing. Neither is predicted to decrease dramatically in the future. Troubleshooters will be seen as one of the most important tools for attacking these problems.

Fifth, since litigation is costing both public and private organizations heavily in terms of money, energy, and time, they are actively searching for alternative means of dispute resolution. In other words, there is a great need for ways of solving problems outside of the courts and the legal system. Pressures from employee and customer litigation costs alone will be extremely conducive to troubleshooter expansion.

Sixth, troubleshooter programs address the organizational problem of "upward feedback." Just how do executives find out what their organizational problems are? Few employees and fewer senior managers tell them, and those who do so comment only at the possible peril of their careers. Troubleshooters create data flow leading to executive education.

Last, as we have seen, the troubleshooter concept now has widespread support. Countries, governments, hospitals, and corporations feel it is an idea that is aligned with the times and the culture. With participative management and industrial democracy gaining in importance, troubleshooter programs are viewed as extremely appropriate.

In this book, I have brought out and defined an innovative concept and process emerging rapidly in organizations in diverse fields. Troubleshooting recognizes that no organizations are perfect. In order to build productivity and to create a high quality of working life and a high quality of consuming life, we must identify, confront, and resolve organizational problems. The use of a troubleshooting program indicates that senior management is aware of the problems in organizations, is willing to take action to correct them, and is attentive to employees' and customers' concerns. Executives and managers with those attitudes we all want to work for.

For all of these reasons, troubleshooters will experience strong support in the present and expansion in the future. The one in your organization will almost certainly be acknowledged or hired in the next five to ten years.

References

Ackoff, R. L. *A Concept of Corporate Planning*. New York: Wiley, 1970.

Ackoff, R. L. *Redesigning the Future*. New York: Wiley, 1974.

Ackoff, R. L. *Creating the Corporate Future*. New York: Wiley, 1981.

Ackoff, R. L. "Participation Within Organizations." *Wharton Alumni Magazine*, Summer, 1985.

Alpert, J. L.., and Meyers, J. *Training in Consultation*. Springfield, Ill.: Thomas, 1983.

Altany, D. R. "Where Customers Rule." *Industry Week*, June 29, 1987, p. 31.

American Hospital Association. Special issue: "Quality Assurance/ Risk Management." *Hospitals*, 1981, 55 (11).

Anderson, S. V. "The Corrections Ombudsman in the United States." In G. E. Caiden (ed.), *International Handbook of the Ombudsman: Evolution and Present Function*. Westport, Conn.: Greenwood Press, 1983.

Annas, G. J., and Healey, J. M. "The Patient Advocate: Redefining the Doctor-Patient Relationship in the Hospital Context." *Vanderbilt Law Review*, 1974, 27, 243–269.

Annas, G. J., Glantz, L. H., and Katz, B. F. *The Rights of Doctors, Nurses, and Allied Health Professionals*. Cambridge, Mass.: Ballinger, 1981.

"The Antiunion Grievance Ploy." *Business Week*, Feb. 12, 1979, p. 117.

Argyris, C., and Schon, D. A. *Theory in Practice: Increasing Professional Effectiveness.* San Francisco: Jossey-Bass, 1975.

Armstrong, J. S. "The Ombudsman: Learner Responsibility in Management Education, or Ventures into Forbidden Research." *Interfaces,* April, 1983, *13* (2), 26–38.

Aufrecht, S. E., and Brelsford, G. "The Administrative Impact of the Alaskan Ombudsman." In G. E. Caiden (ed.), *International Handbook of the Ombudsman: County Surveys.* Westport, Conn.: Greenwood Press, 1983.

Barton, P. M. "Ombudsmanship in Corrections: The Power of Presence on the Prison Premises." In G. E. Caiden (ed.), *International Handbook of the Ombudsman: Evolution and Present Function.* Westport, Conn.: Greenwood Press, 1983.

Below, P. J., Morrisey, G. L., and Acomb, B. L. *The Executive Guide to Strategic Planning.* San Francisco: Jossey-Bass, 1987.

Caiden, G. E. (ed.). *International Handbook of the Ombudsman: Evolution and Present Function.* Westport, Conn.: Greenwood Press, 1983.

Caiden, G. E., MacDermot, N., and Sandler, A. "The Institution of Ombudsman." In Caiden, G. E. (ed.), *International Handbook of the Ombudsman: Evolution and Present Function.* Westport, Conn.: Greenwood Press, 1983.

Capozzola, J. "An American Ombudsman: Problems and Prospects." *Political Quarterly,* 1968, *21,* 289–301.

Carson, S. "People with Gripes Can Find More Ombudsmen." *Montreal Gazette,* 1986, p. F-1.

Clark, K. E. "Improve Employee Relations with a Corporate Ombudsman." *Personnel Journal,* 1985, *64* (9), 12–13.

Clausen, A. W. "Listening and Responding to Employees Concerns." *Harvard Business Review,* 1980.

Cole, D. (ed.). *Conflict Resolution Technology.* Cleveland, Ohio: Organization Development Institute, 1983.

Cutchin, D. A., and Williams, J. O. "Assessing Managerial Behavior in Public Management Students." Paper presented at the annual conference of the American Society for Public Administration, Denver, Colo., Apr. 1984.

Daft, R. L. *Organization Theory and Design.* St. Paul, Minn.: West, 1983.

Danet, B. "Toward a Method to Evaluate the Ombudsman Role." *Administration and Society*, 1978, *10* (3), 335-370.

Davis, L. E., and Cherns, A. B. (eds.). *The Quality of Working Life*. 2 vols. New York: Free Press, 1975.

Deal, T. E., and Kennedy, A. A. *Corporate Cultures: The Rites and Rituals of Corporate Life*. Reading, Mass.: Addison-Wesley, 1982.

Drucker, P. *Management*. New York: Harper & Row, 1973.

Ewing, D. W. "What Business Thinks About Employee Rights." *Harvard Business Review*, 1977, *55* (5).

Ewing, D. W. "An Employee Bill of Rights—A Proposal." In A. F. Westin and S. Salisbury (eds.), *Individual Rights in the Corporation*. New York: Random House, 1980.

Ewing, D. W. *Do It My Way or You're Fired! Employee Rights and the Changing Role of Management Prerogatives*. New York: Wiley, 1983.

Filley, A., and Grimes, A. "The Bases of Power in Decision Processes." *Proceedings of the Annual Meeting of the Academy of Management*, 1967, pp. 133-160.

Filley, A. C., House, R. J., and Kerr, S. *Managerial Process and Organizational Behavior*. Glenview, Ill.: Scott Foresman, 1976.

Foegen, J. H. "Ombudsman as Complement to the Grievance Procedures." *Labor Law Journal*, 1972, *23*, 289-294.

Gellhorn, W. *Ombudsmen and Others: Citizens' Protectors in Nine Counties*. Cambridge, Mass.: Harvard University Press, 1966.

Gwyn, W. B. "Obstacles Within the Office of Economic Opportunity to the Elevation of Experimental Ombudsmen." *Public Administration*, 1975.

Henretta, J. C., and A. O'Roul. "Joint Retirement in the Dual-Worker Family." *Social Forces*, 1983, *62* (2), 504-600.

Hill, L. B. "The Citizen Participation-Representation Roles of American Ombudsmen." *Administration and Society*, 1982, *13* (4), 405-433.

Hill, L. B. "The Self-Perceptions of Ombudsmen: A Comparative Survey." In G. E. Caiden (ed.), *International Handbook of the Ombudsman: Evolution and Present Function*. Westport, Conn.: Greenwood Press, 1983.

Hill, P. *Towards a New Philosophy of Management.* New York: Barnes & Noble, 1971.

Hirschhorn, L., and Krantz, J. "Unconscious Planning in a Natural Work Group: A Case Study in Process Consultation." *Human Relations,* 1982, *35* (10), 805–844.

Hogan, N. S. *Humanizing Health Care: Task of the Patient Representative.* Oradell, N.J.: Medical Economics Company, 1980.

Jacobs, B. A. "Tell It to Bob: Sharp's Ombudsman Smooths Ruffled Feathers." *Industry Week,* 1985, *226,* 62–63.

Jenkins, D. *Job Power: Blue and White Collar Democracy.* New York: Penguin, 1974.

Kaplan, R. E., Drath, W. H., and Kofodimos, J. R. "Power and Getting Criticism." *Issues & Observations* (Center for Creative Leadership, Greensboro, N.C.), 1984, *4* (3), 1–7.

Kast, F. E., and Rosenzweig, J. E. *Organization and Management: A Systems and Contingency Approach.* New York: McGraw-Hill, 1985.

Kiechel, W. "No Word from on High." *Fortune,* Jan. 6, 1986, pp. 125–126.

Laskov, H. "The Military Ombudsman in Israel." In G. E. Caiden (ed.), *International Handbook of the Ombudsman: Evolution and Present Function.* Westport, Conn.: Greenwood Press, 1985.

"Lending an Ear." *Time,* Dec. 7, 1981, p. 62.

Lippit, G. L. "The Trainer's Role as an Internal Consultant." *Journal of European Training,* 1975, *4* (5), 237–246.

Lublin, J. S. "In Britain, Two Women May Lead But Sexism Rules." *Wall Street Journal,* March 13, 1987, p. 1.

McGillis, D. "The Quiet Revolution in American Dispute Settlement." *Harvard Law School Bulletin,* spring 1980, 20–26.

McGillis, D. "Minor Dispute Processing: A Review of Recent Developments." In R. Tomasic and M. Feeley, *Neighborhood Justice.* New York: Longman, 1982.

Meyers, J., Alpert, J. L., and Fleisher, B. D. "Models of Consultation." In J. L. Alpert and J. Meyers, *Training in Consultation.* Springfield, Ill.: Thomas, 1983.

Mitroff, I. *Stakeholders of the Organizational Mind.* San Francisco: Jossey-Bass, 1983.

Naisbitt, J. *Megatrends.* New York: Warner Books, 1982.

Naisbitt, J., and Aburdene, P. *Reinventing the Corporation.* New York: Warner Books, 1985.

Olson, F. C. "How Peer Review Works at Control Data." *Harvard Business Review,* Nov.-Dec. 1984.

Peters, T. J., and Waterman, R. H. *In Search of Excellence.* New York: Warner Books, 1982.

Posavac, E. J., and Carey, R. G. *Program Evaluation: Methods and Case Studies.* Englewood Cliffs, N.J.: Prentice-Hall, 1985.

Pugh, S. "The Ombudsman: Jurisdiction, Powers and Practice." *Public Administration,* 1978, *56,* 127-138.

Ravich, R. "Patient Relations." *Hospitals,* 1975, *49,* 107-109.

Ravich, R., and Rehr, H. "Ombudsman Program Provides Feedback." *Hospitals,* 1974, *48,* 63-67.

Reuss, H. S., and Anderson, S. V. "The Ombudsman: Tribune of the People." *Annals of the American Academy of Political and Social Science,* 1966, *363,* 44-51.

Robbins, L., and Deane, W. B. "The Corporate Ombudsman: A New Approach to Conflict Management." *Negotiation Journal,* 1986, *2* (2), 195-205.

Ross, K. "Providing Staff a Neutral Ear." *Hartford Courant,* Dec. 17, 1986, p. 6.

Rowat, D. "Ombudsman for North America." *Public Administration Review,* 1964, *24,* 226-233.

Rowe, M. P. "The Corporate Ombudsman: An Overview and Analysis." *Negotiation Journal,* 1987, *3* (2), 127-140.

Rowe, M. P., and Baker, M. "Are You Hearing Enough Employee Concerns?" *Harvard Business Review,* 1984, *62* (3), 127-135.

Sandford, J. W. "A Troubleshooter at Fairchild Unit." *New York Times,* 1985, *32.*

Schein, E. H. *Process Consultation: Its Role in Organization Development.* Reading, Mass.: Addison-Wesley, 1969.

Schein, E. H. *Organizational Culture and Leadership.* San Francisco: Jossey-Bass, 1985.

Scheirer, M. A. *Program Implementation: The Organizational Context.* Beverly Hills, Calif.: Sage, 1981.

Shortell, S. M. *Continuing Education for the Health Professions.* Ann Arbor: Health Administration Press, 1978.

Silver, I. "The Corporate Ombudsman." *Harvard Business Review*, May–June 1967, 77–87.

Society of Patient Representatives. *Essentials of Patient Representative Programs in Hospitals*. Chicago: American Hospital Association, 1978.

Steiner, G. A. *Strategic Planning: What Every Manager Must Know*. New York: Free Press, 1979.

Tillier, E. "A Man for All Reasons." *The Bank's World*, Mar. 1987, 15–18.

Trist, E. *The Evolution of Sociotechnical Systems*. Toronto: Quality of Working Life Center, June 1981.

Umstot, D. D., Mitchell, T. R., and Bell, C. H. "Goal Setting and Job Enrichment: An Integrated Approach to Job Design." *Academy of Management Review*, Oct. 1978, 877.

Verkuil, P. R. "The Ombudsman and the Limits of the Adversary System." *Columbia Law Review*, 1975, 75, 845–861.

Vollmer, H. M., and Mills, D. (eds.). *Professionalization*. Englewood Cliffs, N.J.: Prentice-Hall, 1966.

Weber, M. *The Theory of Social and Economic Organizations*, trans. by A. M. Henderson and Talcott Parsons. Fairlawn, N.J.: Oxford University Press, 1947.

Weiss, C. H. "Use of Social Science Research in Organizations: The Constraints Repertoire Theory." In H. D. Stein (ed.), *Organization and the Human Services*. Philadelphia: Temple University Press, 1981.

Westin, A. F., and Salisbury, S. (eds.). *Individual Rights in the Corporation*. New York: Pantheon Books, 1980.

Ziegenfuss, D. G., and Ziegenfuss, J. T. *Health Information Systems: A Bibliography*. New York: Plenum Press, 1984.

Ziegenfuss, J. T. "Responding to People Problems." *Business Horizons*, 1980, 23 (2), 73–76.

Ziegenfuss, J. T. "Do Your Managers Think in Organizational 3-D?" *Sloan Management Review*, 1982, 24 (1), 55–59.

Ziegenfuss, J. T. *Patient's Rights and Organizational Models: Socio-Technical Systems Research on Mental Health Programs*. Washington, D.C.: University Press of America, 1983a.

Ziegenfuss, J. T. *Patients' Rights and Professional Practice*. New York: Van Nostrand Reinhold, 1983b.

Ziegenfuss, J. T. *DRGs and Hospital Impact: An Organizational Systems Analysis.* New York: McGraw-Hill, 1985a.

Ziegenfuss, J. T. "Handling Employee Complaints." *Employee Services Management,* 1985b, *28* (4), 26–29.

Ziegenfuss, J. T. *Patient/Client/Employee Complaint Programs: An Organizational Systems Model.* Springfield, Ill.: Thomas, 1985c.

Ziegenfuss, J. T. "Corporate Complaint Programs Make Gains from Gripes." *Personnel Journal,* 1987, *66* (4), 40–42.

Ziegenfuss, J. T., and Lasky, D. I. "Evaluation and Organizational Development: A Management Consulting Approach." *Evaluation Review,* 1980a, *4* (5), 665–676.

Ziegenfuss, J. T., Charette, J., and Guenin, M. "The Patients' Rights Representative Program: Design of an Ombudsman Service for Mental Patients." *Psychiatric Quarterly,* 1984, *56* (1), 3–12.

Ziegenfuss, J. T., Robbins, L., and Rowe, M. *Corporate Ombudsmen: An Exploratory National Survey of Purposes and Activities.* Center for the Quality of Working Life, Pennsylvania State University, Harrisburg, Pa., and Corporate Ombudsman Association, 1987.

Index